Reviews for Catherine
which served as the fou

"Every bit as challenging, erfully written from the heart, she develops key gospel themes.... This work is mandatory reading for anyone who is attempting to live the values of Jesus Christ today."

— Steve Coffey, *Book Nook*

"There is no watering down of the gospel's revolutionary message. An almost terrible urgency characterizes this book: the time is now to choose between the death to self, the opening of out hearts to Christ's life and to people, and the death of our souls from loneliness, fear and the 'deifications of man.'... in her vigorous and incisive expression of these truths of the gospel, they take on new meanings, greater clarity and depth.... It is the author's singular ability to make one confront oneself...that gives the book its power."

— Maureen Gorman, *St. Anthony Messenger*

"An excellent book to pick up and read a few pages at a time. Each chapter... suggests some matter for spiritual reflection.... Everyone striving to live a truly Christian life will benefit from *The Gospel Without Compromise*."

— Father Daniel A. Hurley, O.F.M., M.A., *The Cord*

"Like everything from her pen, this latest book by Catherine Doherty is touchingly simple, straight from the heart, and very wise.... Her years of total dedication to the people of God, the crosses she has carried, and the tremendous graces she has received all leave their mark on what she writes, adding new depths now to the perception which has always been hers.... a present-day prophet whose commission is validated by a long life spent in 'living the Gospel without compromise.'"

— Sister Marie Emmanuel S.C., *Sisters Today*

"This is a very down-to-earth and straightforward book that leaves us little place to hide in rationalizations or excuses. It is also a very good book to help us honestly look at our lives and how we are following the Gospel. I highly recommend it for all Christians."

— Sharon Martorana, *Charism Canada*

"The Christian message is applied unsparingly to service on the contemporary social scene which makes it challenging and motivating reading."

— *Today's Parish*

Living The Gospel Without Compromise

Catherine de Hueck Doherty

Compiled by Marian Heiberger

Madonna House Publications
Combermere, Ontario, Canada

Madonna House Publications®
2888 Dafoe Rd
Combermere ON K0J 1L0

www.madonnahouse.org/publications

Living the Gospel Without Compromise
by Catherine de Hueck Doherty (née Kolyschkine)
© 2002 Madonna House Publications. All rights reserved.

No part of this work may be reproduced, stored in a retrieval system or transmitted in any form or by any means, electronic, mechanical, or otherwise, without express written permission. The Our Lady of Combermere colophon is a registered trade-mark of Madonna House Publications.

First Edition

First printing, September 11th, 2002.

Printed in Canada

Edited by Marian Heiberger and Martin Nagy

Parts of this work previously appeared in the book *The Gospel Without Compromise* by Catherine Doherty, published by Ave Maria Press in 1976 and Madonna House Publications in 1989.

Scripture quotations are taken from the New Jerusalem Bible, copyright © 1985 by Darton, Longman & Todd, London, and Doubleday, a division of Random House, Inc., New York.

Design by Rob Huston

This book is set in Berkeley Oldstyle, designed by Frederic W. Goudy for the University of California Press in 1938. Heading text is set in Rotis SemiSerif, designed by Otl Aicher for Agfa in 1989.

National Library of Canada Cataloguing in Publication Data

Doherty, Catherine de Hueck, 1896–1985
   Living the Gospel without compromise / Catherine Doherty ; compiled by Marian Heiberger

ISBN 0-921440-86-3

   1. Christian life—Catholic authors. 2. Christian life—Biblical teaching.   I. Heiberger, Marian. II. Title.

BX2350.3.D633 2002   248.4   C2002-904589-4

No one can have greater love
than to lay down his life for his friends.

John 15:13

Contents

Foreword 9
1. Holy Insecurity 11
2. The Sign of Love 21
3. Sacrifice 29
4. The Church and Renewal 35
5. Community 43
6. Modern Society 51
7. Christian Culture 65
8. My Brother's Keeper 71
9. Evangelization 79
10. Ecumenical Bridges 93
11. Unity in the Trinity 101
12. The Sacraments 107
13. Stewardship 121
14. Living with Danger 125
15. Overcoming Fear 129
16. Nonviolence 133
17. Faith 139
18. Hope 145
19. Love 149
    About the Author 155

Foreword

In this day and age we have been called to struggle, through gospel living and a new evangelization, against the culture of death and toward the culture of life. This is the battle: Will we choose to love as Christ loves or will we not. We are all called to the battle. Catherine Doherty envisioned and heeded Christ's call to the laity to carry out this apostolate of love throughout the world.

The words of Pope John Paul II confirm Catherine's labours. He has said to us, "We are living in the time of the laity. The laity is indispensable for an adequate response to the present needs of evangelization. This is not just an operational need because of the decrease in religious vocations. It is a new and hitherto unheard of possibility that God is granting us."

Throughout her apostolic life, Catherine, by example and word, equipped the laity for carrying out this calling of our times. Through the writings compiled in this book, Catherine shares some of the catechesis of her own heart. The chapters on ecumenism and on the sacraments have been augmented with quotes from official sources, including the *Catechism of the Catholic Church* and *The Documents of Vatican II*. This is a down-to-earth handbook for catechizing our own hearts—equipping us for everyday Christian living in the midst of the dramatic climate of our world.

Originally written years ago, Catherine's mention of terrorism in this book now seems prophetic. The terrorist attacks of September 11, 2001 have compounded our already complicated lives. We live our lives in the midst of pending terror, technological depersonalization, new age spiritualism, atheistic philosophy, and celebrated materialism. We seem to be taxed to the limit over the concerns pressing upon our world, our Church, and our everyday lives with Christ, family, and community.

We can use Catherine's words and experiences to interiorize the new evangelization, so that we can bring life to people in this mechanistic society by simply living ordinary Christian lives in the marketplace. Jesus tells us that the single-minded, the pure in heart, will see God. *Living the Gospel Without Compromise* is a handbook for single-minded living through the chaotic distractions and disparate conditions of our times.

Catherine addresses our concerns—danger, security, the rapid changes in the world, the culture of death, sin, our need for dignity, healing, unity, Christian culture, the culture of life. She addresses all these with simplicity. She shows us that ordinary, everyday Christianity is simply following Jesus in laying down our lives for others. She shows us that the simple answer to bringing healing to those around us, to changing the world, is simply living the gospel—without compromise.

— the editors

Chapter 1

Holy Insecurity

> How blessed are you who are poor:
> the kingdom of God is yours.
>
> Luke 6:20

These days people are teetering on the edge of an abyss, with the threat of terrorism in the background. The security to which most people cling is mere illusion. We are not secure walking the streets of a large modern city. In planes, we never know if we'll stay up or not. Wars flare up in almost every part of the world. So where is the security that we seem to value so dearly?

God doesn't give us this material security. He offers instead faith, a faith which begins, in a sense, where reason ends.

Security begins when we love God with our whole heart, mind, and soul, and our neighbour as ourselves.

We must, like Christ, be paradoxical. Christ said, "All who draw the sword will die by the sword," (Matthew 26:52) but he also said, "It is not peace I have come to bring, but a sword." (Matthew 10:34) Paradox!

Nothing upsets our civilization more than the paradox surrounding security. We don't want risk and insecurity. But choosing a security that doesn't follow Christ can be killing us, spiritually.

God offers us risk, danger, and an insecurity that leads to perfect security. His security begins when we start loving God with our whole heart, our whole mind, and our whole soul, and our neighbour as ourselves. This can never be overstressed. If we do not clothe our lives with his love, we shall perish.

To love one's neighbour is the ultimate risk. It may even mean death for my brother's sake. For this kind of loving, we have the Holy Spirit in us. With his help, we shall be able to love our neighbour. With him, we shall have the courage to risk loving our neighbour. It is a tremendous risk, because we are also asked by Christ to love our enemies. Once we have entered into Christ's command to love as he loved us, (John 15:12) we have the power and grace, the charisms, to change enemies into friends and beloved neighbours.

All this sounds very idealistic and perhaps quite unobtainable. Christ assures us it is attainable. It is through little steps taken day after day that one slowly accepts the other as he or she is, and begins to love totally, tenderly, compassionately.

Why settle for a pale reflection of Christ's teachings?

Christ calls each one of us. He calls us directly. There is no compromise in his call: "Anyone who is not with me is against me." (Matthew 12:30) "You are my friends, if you do what I command you." (John 15:14) We can find umpteen quotations in the gospel that will vividly bring to our minds and hearts how simply and insistently Christ calls us to become like him and to accept his law of love without compromises.

Why do we not try the way of love, the way of the gospel? Why do we not apply the gospel without compromise to our personal, national, and international lives?

To solve our problems we seem to have tried everything that our intelligence and genius can come up with. But so far, if we are to be judged by the fruits of the tree, (Matthew 7:16–20) we certainly have not succeeded. Nor are we leaving our children a better world to live in. On the contrary, we are leaving them an even more chaotic world than the one we inherited.

The answers to our problems, however, rest in the gospel. How simple and how timely it is! It is like a light shining in the darkness. Why is it then that we who are Christians refuse to even try the clear answers of the gospel? Why do we wish to constantly compromise, water down, and eliminate from the gospel whatever is too hard for us? Why settle for a pale reflection of Christ's strong words and loving teachings?

It is imperative that we go back to the source of all things—the gospel. Many people read books about the gospel much more than they read the gospel itself. Their knowledge of the Glad News may be fairly superficial. Before we can proclaim the gospel with our lives, we need to know the gospel, to read the gospel.

The gospel can be summed up by saying that it is the tremendous, tender, compassionate, gentle, extraordinary, explosive, revolutionary law of Christ's love. Christ calls us to become like him. But what did he do? In the gospel, we hear that the people wanted to make him king, because he gave them material things—fed them bread and fishes, raised the dead, cured the sick. But he fled, out of their way, for his kingdom is not of this world. (John 6:5–15) To the contrary, Jesus did his greatest work when he was nailed to a cross, helpless, unable to give anyone anything except love and his life. This redeemed us.

Do not hide the price that you pay for living the gospel, because this gives hope to others.

Whether living in humble apartments, suburban homes, or palatial dwellings, people are talking about God. Their minds are preoccupied with his strange and eternal fascination. Do they deny him? They cannot do it calmly. Do they accept him? Some accept him with great passion. Alas, in most instances, those who say they believe in him are lukewarm and far from passionate in their expression, as if they were not quite sure of themselves. There is no dynamism, no Pentecostal fire burning in them.

But certain signs of an awakening are becoming visible. Today many Christians are coming to the poor more as servants than as benefactors. And many people are turning to prayer.

Yet something seems to be still missing—a vibrant, passionate totality of commitment. What is missing is a cry out of the very depths of our souls for an increase of faith that would transcend all limits of time and space. What is missing is the vision that faces every event of life in the light of Christ's teaching. What is missing is a discernment that distinguishes between a security that depends on ourselves and the security of faith which is the heritage of the Christian.

Cast your eyes around the whole world. So many people still don't know Jesus' name. Let's face it. If the world is atheistic—if much of it has not yet heard the Good News or has not accepted it, then the main fault lies with us Christians who have not lived the gospel. We have watered down the gospel message.

Christianity became an affair of ethical, moral behavior; of going to church; of learning rules to get to heaven. The gap between the reality of the gospel and the watered down teaching is reaping its harvest of damage.

The Christian problem is not that we seem to be living in *diaspora*. The problem is that we Christians do not understand that the world is always hungry for the reality that is Christ. There is a massive search for God taking place—the God of Christians. People are searching for the carpenter of Nazareth, the poor itinerant preacher, the God-man who died for love of us.

Perhaps it seems a bit farfetched to say that young rebels are pilgrims of the Absolute, that those who take drugs are searching for God. But many of us know this is so, because we meet them constantly and listen endlessly to their hunger for spiritual things, for a meaning in life. We see in their confusion the eye of the hurricane.

Today, across a confused world, people seek the real Christ, the Christ of the gospel, the one people have read about but cannot seem to find. In their seeking, people ask, "How can I find Christ? Why does he seem to be so illusive, so unreal, so difficult to meet?" It seems to me that the answer to these questions is exceedingly simple—we meet Christ in a real Christian.

What a strange and seemingly simplistic answer. Yet, it is the true answer. I don't think there is another. People have to be shown. The time of mere talking is over.

After his resurrection, Christ showed his disciples his wounds and they believed. These wounds were visible signs of Christ's love for them and for all of us. No one needed to say anything, least of all Christ. Thomas the Doubter was the only one who spoke. (John 20:24–29)

We must likewise show the wounds of Christ to others, for then they will believe. This is what people are seeking today—someone who will show them the wounds of Christ so that they may touch him and be reassured. How do we get those wounds? By living the gospel without compromise. For we who follow a crucified God, are also called to be crucified. It is important that we do not hide from each other the price that we have to pay for living the gospel, because this gives hope to others.

Empty your heart of all the things that are not God.

Yet we ought to go further. Christ prepared breakfast on the beach for his friends. (John 21:12) We, too, by our service, can show how much we love our brethren, all those who are seeking the Lord.

But even all this—to show the wounds, to prepare meals—is not enough. One can symbolically open one's heart with a lance, by taking that lance into one's own hands, so as to become able to accept all human beings as they are, without wanting to change or to manipulate them. That we are together is a benediction and a joy in itself.

People will not know God unless we, their neighbours, their brethren, show Christ to them with his own tremendous love. Then they may once again say what was said of the early Christians, "See how these Christians love one another."

We are called to open the doors of our hearts and to open the doors of our homes. It is essential that we accept people as they are, and that we serve them, and that we show them the wounds of our love. Love is always wounded because love and pain are inseparable. Even as a young woman barely falling in love is worried about her boyfriend traveling on a snowy road to Chicago, so in the love of people for each other, pain is interwoven. There is no love without pain.

But how do we acquire these wounds that we are called to show? Where do we get the strength to cook supper for someone when we ourselves are already exhausted by the day's toil? How do we get strength to open the doors of our heart which we so readily want to close against the noise of our incredibly noisy world?

Let's face it. We cannot love the way we ought to. God alone can love us that way. So we need to empty our hearts of all the things that are not God. By emptying ourselves according to his commandments of love, and with his grace, we can allow God to love in us.

The Lord commanded us to love our enemies. Until we do, we cannot show Christ to others. We are asked to lay down our lives for our brethren. Words are not enough. But a loving glance, a wound, a breakfast cooked for a friend, a welcome through an open door into an open heart, these will do it. It is only then, when my brother has been filled with my supper, when he has beheld my wounds of love for him, when he has experienced a totality of acceptance, only then will he be open to glad news.

Humanity today is the "Doubting Thomas" who wasn't there when Christ appeared to the apostles after his resurrection. Humanity today needs to touch the wounds of Christ in order to believe, to be converted. Then, people will come to the Lord in thousands, perhaps in millions.

Does living the gospel mean demolishing our comfortable way of life?

The only way to show these wounds of Christ to others is to live the gospel without compromise. Does that mean that we must turn our lives upside down? Does it mean a complete change of values? Does it mean breaking up, demolishing our comfortable way of life? Quite simply, yes, it does.

It would be better to stop calling ourselves Christians—followers of Christ who is Love—than to scandalize our brothers and sisters by going through the motions of being Christians, rendering lip service only.

When we who call ourselves Christians show forth the gospel in our lives, then the searchers for God, these pilgrims of the Absolute, will see him and touch him, and they will believe.

It is time that we show people the face of the resurrected Christ in whom we and all creation have our being. It's time that we cease to bemoan our miseries and begin to love one another, to form communities of love to which all others can come—communities where people can touch, see, and feel the wounds of Christ. We who work in the front lines of spiritual warfare know that this is the only answer for a world which seeks so desperately for meaning in life.

People are bewildered by the insatiable greed of the military complex. We find intolerable the monotony of the assembly line that kills our spirit. Bewilderment continues as we see the waste of world resources. These and other questions have coalesced into one: "Who is God?"

People are slowly beginning to understand that only through God and only by living his command to love will the problems of our tragic days be solved—only by a love that is face to face, person to person. This is the moment for us who call ourselves Christians to begin facing one another on a one-to-one basis. Each person needs to know that he or she is loved, loved as a friend, loved as a brother or sister in Christ. This can only be done person to person. It cannot be done *en masse*.

It is only in the eyes of another, in the face of another, that we can find the icon or image of Christ. There are many ways of praising God, many ways of praying to him, many ways of searching for him. But today there is one great way, one profound way, one gentle, tender, and compassionate way. It is by a person-to-person love. We can make the other aware that we love him. If we do, he will know that God loves him.

Following Christ means living dangerously.

We are required to openly declare either our allegiance to Christ or nonallegiance to him. The story of the disciples who had to choose repeats itself among us. Jesus asked, "Who do you say that I am?" (Matthew 16:15) Peter, replying for himself and the other apostles, openly declared himself for Jesus. It is time we do likewise and stop fooling around.

Many of the disciples found Christ's words too hard, admitted it, and left him. (John 6:67) It is time for us to face God and tell him either, "Yes, Lord, we are with you, for where else can we go?" or, "No,

Lord, your sayings are too hard, and we will not follow you any longer."

A sense of deep sadness comes over me when I think of how Christians sit on the fence. What is the matter with us? Have we forgotten that we are followers of a crucified Christ? Have we forgotten that from the moment he began preaching, he walked in the shadow of death? Have we forgotten that following him means taking the greatest risk that anyone can take? Have we forgotten that following him means living dangerously?

It seems that we have spent centuries trying to eliminate the risk and the danger of his call. It seems that we have cushioned the risk and practically eliminated any and all danger by drawing up a set of moral rules that allow us to feel a human security instead of the holy insecurity Christ calls us to—rules that lull our conscience to sleep instead of making it wide awake and ready to undertake the risks of being a Christian.

Christ said that if we are not with him, we are against him. (Luke 11:23) How do we measure up to this saying of his? Are we really with him? Are we ready to give up father, mother, sister, and brother, in the sense he means it, as following him demands? Are we ready to lay our lives on the line of his law of love with its fantastic dimensions of dispossession and surrender? Do we truly love one another, beginning with ourselves? God is not mocked. How long can we sit on the fence of compromise?

When you are rejected for Christ's sake, you become one with him.

The gospel of Christ is magnificent in its beauty and inexorable in its demands. The gospel of Christ is also gentle as a breeze in the spring but terrible as the cross. The gospel sometimes becomes for me one single sentence: No one can have greater love than to lay down his life for his fellowmen. (John 15:13)

The immense problems of war, of social injustice, of the thousand-and-one ills that beset our world can be solved only if we begin to love one another. When people begin to see love, respect and reverence in the eyes of another, then they will change and society will change, also. If ever there was a time when humanity needed followers of Christ and fewer fence-sitters, that time is now.

The world is crying for the Bread of Life, for the living waters that Christ promised—for God himself. But Christians who possess the bread and the living waters do not know how to share the bread they eat. They forget that whoever eats the Bread of the Lord is required to be "eaten up" by others. Having received God who is love, we must give love. Unless we love and show Christ's face to those around us we have wasted our lives.

You and I cannot say that we did not hear the gospel, that we do not know it. We did hear it, but we do not want to act on it. One reason is that if we do we shall be rejected by our peers. But the person who is thus rejected becomes one with Christ.

We must begin to love one another in the fullest sense of Christ's teaching. To do so it is urgent that we pray. It is only through prayer that we can follow Christ to Golgotha and end up being suspended on the other side of his cross, that we can become free through this "ascension."

Christ is still being crucified in his Mystical Body, in his people, but he is alive. He was raised from the dead. He is God, and he lives in us and will continue to love us until our last breath, no matter how we feel about him. Christ reigns supreme over everyone, over all the world of creatures, over all the universes that man has discovered or will discover. The Galilean will conquer again and again.

Christ's commandments imply that we need to let go of the security that we still cling to.

Charity, or love, can be resurrected in the hearts of persons if only they will stop and think about love, about God, about the incredible fact that God loved them first, and that all they have to do to banish strife, wars, bombs, suspicions, doubts, and fears, is to begin to love him back and to love all their neighbours. Then the light and fire of charity will be so immense that no one will have to fear either bombs or the hatred of his brother.

It is time we Christians awoke from our long sleep. It is time we shed our indifference toward God. Then, we shall know true peace, true joy. The answers to our international and national problems will become clear in proportion to our love.

Christ's call is revolutionary, there is no denying it. If we Christians would put it into practice it would change the world in a few months. The gospel is radical, and Christ indeed is the radix, the root from which all things spring. His commandments require risk, great risk. They infer an absence of that security that most of us so tightly cling to.

Chapter 2

The Sign of Love

*I have come to bring fire to the earth,
and how I wish it were blazing already!*

Luke 12:49

The Church is called to be present in this world as a sign of love. The Church needs to meet each person right where he or she lives, in the fundamental core of his or her life.

Changes have come to our world where millions of people do not even bother with any kind of religion, let alone the Christian religion. It seems to me that it will take many years for theology to catch up with these changes that our technological civilization faces—automation and space programs, changes in this pluralistic society that make communications faster than sound, changes that make the world become one mechanically. But who will bring forth motives that enable people to work toward making the world become one in brotherhood, and save it from self-destruction? Who can prevent contemporary man from his ultimate failure: falling victim to the myth of Prometheus—deifying himself?

It seems to me that it will be done by the Church meeting contemporary people in the center of that sign of love which it is meant to be. The Church needs to participate in all the stages of changes that humanity passes through. This applies to everything—technology, science, the existing organizations in the world, anything that tries to meet the needs of people today.

God has given each person the mission to not be separated from the other. This demands something tremendous from all of us Christians, especially Catholics. It demands that we abandon a limited outlook and the narrow vision that many Christians tend to box all human problems into.

Listen to all the mixed voices of humanity.

This is a wonderful time in which to be alive, but it is also a time to think, in the full sense of this explosive word. We are called to be master listeners who listen to the people of God and to the hierarchy but also to the mixed voices of humanity—atheist, Protestant, Jew, Muslim, to the voices of all the minorities and majorities.

It takes effort to avoid the pitfall of superficial communications. After listening, we have to digest what we've heard. Our evaluating is not to be boxed into abstract ideas, as interesting and profitable as this might be. Rather we need to digest, appraise, evaluate, synthesize in a particular manner. When discussing what we have heard, we are all urged to rise to the challenge of creating a climate that is objective, leaving behind our individual and emotional sensitivities. We need to season our listening with constant prayer and much fasting, so that with the help of the Holy Spirit we may discern what applies to our group or community. Then we will see how the results of this intellectual and spiritual activity fit into the tremendous spiritual wealth within our reach.

We need to project ourselves into each situation. We need to study the current issues. We have a duty to be alert and awake. We cannot be indifferent anymore.

Become an icon of Christ.

We are up against a situation that demands heroism. Are we going to live the gospel without compromise or are we going to compromise? To put it in a different way, are we going to think things over in a nice, prudent way? Are we going to use human prudence or the prudence of God? Human prudence evades the cross, or at least puts a foam rubber cushion on it for ourselves. The prudence of God is the folly of the cross.

We are at the crossroads of history, and on our decision, our collective decision, depend many people, and perhaps in some way, the Church. Today faith hangs in the balance, the faith of countless people.

Christ loves us so much that he died for us. How is it possible that we can let go of anybody that he put in our path of life, without showing them that Christ loves them? I am concerned that even one person may not know Christ, because I haven't shown him the way. We have a choice.

People will not believe that God loves them unless they see it in our eyes. We are each called to become an icon of Christ. Are we going to go all out for Christ? Once we agree to this, once we really believe that we can take two fishes and five loaves and feed the multitude, then we see that we ourselves are going to be the bread and the fish that they are going to eat. This is almost certain. Here we have to trust that God will give us what we need.

The entire world, the Church, and all mankind are stepping onto a bridge. There is no turning back! What has been a cultural and historical reality is reaching a climax. The old order is dead and no one can see clearly how nations and cultures will deal with cataclysmic changes.... Humility, littleness, hiddenness are the only weapons we will have in the days ahead.

Jean Fox
Inflamed by Love

There is no love without pain—take the knife of charity and open yourself.

We are at the crossroads. Many in Canada and America haven't enough background in history and such to understand what is coming. We need to be together, so as to stand against what is coming. We need to figure things out. At the same time, we need to say, "I believe and I accept the gospel." Christ will be in our midst. We need faith, faith expressed from a trembling heart, perhaps, but faith. Is our collective conscience willing to accept the gospel, to try it and see?

I'm talking about the inner self that can create peace or war, goodness or badness. It's what goes out of me, not what comes into me. We may be put under a tremendous strain with regard to that inner self. We need to overcome our cultural expectations. This is heroic for Westerners. We need to take the knife of charity and open ourselves. This openness of heart means surrendering "my" for the sake of "our."

Christ presented these laws of love to us:

"Love God....love your neighbour as yourself." (Matthew 22:37–39)

"It is by your love for one another, that everyone will recognize you as my disciples." (John 13:35)

"Love your enemies." (Matthew 5:44)

"No one can have greater love than to lay down his life for his friends." (John 15:13)

These are exemplified and enlarged over and over again in the gospel. Do we really believe Christ's laws of love? What have we done with them? Have we forgotten that they have political and social implications? It is not enough for us to just love one another. Our love must, somehow or other, absolutely must, impenetrate, incarnate itself into the world.

The Lord desires us to be united in one body under his head, in the unity of love. But for us to passionately love God and others, both individually and on a human level, we are required to open our heart to the gospel and to its pain. There is no love without pain.

I am called to lay my life down to rectify the injustices that I meet. We are useless as a tool in God's hand if we do not love one another, day by day, prayer by prayer, hour by hour. "You are the light of the world," he says. (Matthew 5:14) Because we love one another, we become a light. The Holy Spirit illuminates us. We are full of light if we love one another.

Being full of light, we attract others. It's not us, but God in us that attracts others to come and see what is this light that shines in the darkness. Then, we can become the people of the towel and water. Christ knelt down and washed the feet of his apostles (John 13: 1–15). That's a physical act, an act that all of us Christians can do. Sometimes tears are mingled with the water.

This is Christianity. Can you find it? Where is it? Is Canada Christian? Is America Christian? Or do greed, selfishness, desire for profit, individualism at the expense of the other rule our national life?

But what's the use of talking about it if I haven't developed a conscience? And how does one develop one's conscience? That's very simple. We go back to love again. Through concern for the other we become aware of a lot of things.

Embrace everyone.

Shaping the future means changing myself constantly so that I truly become the icon or image of Christ, so that when you look at my face or I look at yours, we know that we are loved. In your eyes and my eyes, people see the eyes of Christ and are comforted.

We have to retrench. We have to act differently, to think differently, to approach life differently. We have to become a fire. We have to be inside of the faith that God has given us. Jump into faith like you jump into the water. It's not only that we have to have faith, we must be inside of it. You pray to God so that you will become an oasis and people will come to you.

We have to watch for the temptation to try to establish God's kingdom by human means, or social action from private initiative. We're inclined to build our own hospitals, schools, and so on, with emphasis on "our own." Each human being individually and all collectively are obliged to cooperate with everyone, with other Christian religions, with social reforms. As that sign of love, which the Church is in this world, we are called to embrace everyone. We cannot think of building only for our own. We are urged to blend with all the forces of a given community in order to effect the immense changes that are demanded of those who love and those who need.

This sign of love must begin with ourselves. We Christians are commanded to love one another. As the sign of love becomes evident in our love for one another, spilling over into every nook and corner of our modern world, then we can begin to preach the word with our voices. We can begin to preach the word with our voices, because we have first preached it with our lives. We have broken down the invisible walls of the past which kept us from being a sign of love.

Isn't the Church a community of love, of faith, and of worship? But how is anyone to find out that it is a community of faith and worship if no one knows it as a community of love? When the whole

Church, hierarchical and lay, becomes a sign of love, then those who do not belong to its community of faith and worship may want to do so, because we will have incarnated the word. Our sign of love will be palpable and visible, as were the wounds of Christ to the apostle Thomas.

Build communities of love.

The Catholic Church is in grave danger because of the cold hearts of so-called Christians. We treat the Church as if it were only human. Many of us are tearing it apart, getting it down to our human level, treating it as if it were just another organization or institution, and forgetting the awesome fact that it is also and predominantly an organism, a body, the head of which is Christ. We are crucifying Christ again in ourselves. We totally forget the awesomeness of the mystery of the Church.

It came to me that God has been giving signs of warning to us, writing on seen and unseen walls, awesome words of warning of the calamities besetting the world. We easily explain away those of nature, but I mean also the terrible, unholy wars men rage one against the other in their souls. The people of God are divided, fragmented. The gospel is rejected in the most obvious ways, in startling, fearsome clarity. Many have become reformers, not according to the Spirit of the Lord, but according to their own spirit, often impregnated with the Spirit of Evil.

I fully understand the words of God that the Church will continue to exist and that hell will not prevail against it. (Matthew 16:18) But it also seems to me that we, the Catholics at large, as seen and heard through our media, through all the turmoil that exists now, are slowly but surely driving that Church, already in the *Diaspora,* into the catacombs.

I shudder at the responsibility of my brothers and sisters in Christ and my own. The ones who tear the Church apart are our elite, people endowed by God with beyond average intelligence and talents. I tremble at the misuse of those talents and the shirking of the true responsibility that these talents give. For the gospel says, woe to those who scandalize the little ones of Christ. (Luke 17:1–3)

The future could be exceedingly dark, depending on how many just people God will find amongst us. (Genesis 18:22–32) By "just" I mean, in this case, loving. People who love their enemies. People who love each other and God. We need to build communities of love. It seems to me that this is God's answer, his loving answer, to the chaos that we have created, to the ignoring of the essentials of the gospel, to the terrible increase in violence in our days.

Having listened to people from developing countries, I realize there is one thing that the world needs today, and that is a group of persons who live the gospel. For the world wants to see and touch, as the Apostle Thomas, the wounds of Christ—because where there is love there are wounds. Christ is the bond, the love-bond, that wants to bind us together.

Chapter 3

Sacrifice

If anyone wants to be a follower of mine, let him renounce himself and take up his cross every day and follow me.

Luke 9:23

During the night recently I entered into the stillness of faith and was listening for God to speak. It seemed that the Lord said to me, "Think." Then he put before me an immense dilemma, a sort of insoluble state of affairs.

On one side of the dilemma, I saw thousands, millions, perhaps billions of people occupying the earth, so that the whole earth seemed covered with people; they were shoulder to shoulder with other persons. This picture seemed to resolve itself into the conclusion that there are too many people with too little land. Too many people with too little land and no food, because so many could not till the land. Moreover, the land was already untillable, because cities sprawled themselves across it, and because the land was polluted by pesticides and the remnants of all sorts of chemicals, some of them exceedingly dangerous, including remnants of nuclear waste.

On the other side of the dilemma, mighty people laboured to preserve life. One by one, diseases were abolished, and the number of people increased because of this. I looked at this and shivered, because something was missing, was out of kilter. I thought of all that has been said about the fact that God does not want sickness or ugliness to touch his beloved people. A voice seemed to come out of the past, the voice that sent the first two people out of the garden of

Eden. An angel with a flaming sword is said to stand guarding the gate of that garden. (Genesis 3:24) The voice said that women will give birth to children in pain. And men will die. (Genesis 3:16, 19) This had the ring of truth to it. I knew that at the very moment the voice ceased speaking, suffering had entered the world.

Then, I heard the sound of nails driven into human flesh. As in a movie, I saw in a flicker of time the whole thing—the Yes of Mary assenting to become the Mother of God, God's incarnation and birth, his time in the carpenter's shop, his departure from home and the preaching of his gospel, Gethsemane, his being bound and sent to Caiphas and then to Pilate.

When I heard nails entering the flesh, I realized that suffering had come to a point, a fantastic, incredible point. I had to either believe or leave faith behind and never believe again.

I believed. I believed that because God the Father loved us, loved the human race so much, he gave his only Son over to suffering, to death on the cross. This is beyond the understanding of any human being, because we do not know what love is, and how pain and love are joined together.

I was confronted with this situation. The answer to people standing shoulder to shoulder on the earth ostensibly seemed rather simple—birth control, abortion, and euthanasia. All three stood before me and nodded their heads, as if they were right there, witnesses at some kind of trial, whose verdict they agreed to fully.

But I didn't agree. I knew there had to be something else, some other answer. I realized that we Christians had yet another task to perform. Beginning with ourselves, our own community, we had to teach a new lifestyle. Perhaps it wasn't new. Perhaps it was centuries old. We had to teach continence to people—the restraint which a person imposes upon his passions and sexuality—and a new lifestyle, where man has freedom to till his earth, to eat its fruits, where one loves God and loves his or her spouse, with a great love. Continence is the fruit of love. Only true love is continent. We have to teach by our example how to live again, instead of to just "exist."

Then I returned to the immense question of suffering. For here were doctors and scientists and faith healers eliminating suffering. This cannot be the ultimate goal. If God sent his only Son to redeem us through suffering, then suffering has a place in our lives.

Sacrifice

Suffering has many edges. One can offer oneself, even as Christ did, as a victim soul—offer oneself to suffer for others. One can offer one's suffering life to God like St. Paul, who said, "It makes me happy to be suffering for you now, and in my own body to make up all the hardships that still have to be undergone by Christ for the sake of his body, the Church." (Colossians 1:24)

Cry out to lift the cross, carry it.

When God has for many years taken one by the hand, as it were, and gently showed one the real value of all things, and then showered one with gift after gift—supreme gifts like suffering and pain, sorrow and loneliness, persecution and misunderstandings that hurt so deeply—one comes to appreciate the meaning of St. Paul's teaching.

Christ seemed to show me the depths of his heart as he walked the way of the cross, as he endured the kiss of Judas; the depths of his heart in Gethsemane, in his cry to his Father asking, "If it is possible, let this cup pass me by." (Matthew 26:39) And I understood that we will do the same as he did. We will cry out to lift the cross, we will carry it, because we believe. We will be open to ridicule on all sides because anyone who does things like allowing oneself to be kissed by Judas will be ridiculed. Christ was ridiculed on the cross and still is, even now.

There are plenty of people ready to save the world in easy ways, but these easy ways don't work. There are a few…who both realize that they can save the world only by suffering, and have the tenacity of purpose to carry their self-sacrifice through. Their success is completely out of proportion to their numbers. These are the people who convert the world.

Father Paul Hanley Furfey, S.J., in a letter of spiritual direction to Catherine

It seems as if the world needs fools—fools for Christ! Fools for God's sake. For it is such fools that have changed the face of the earth.

We are called to sacrifice.

When Carter was president he called the U.S.A. to sacrifice. He called for restraint and unselfishness along the physical lines of our life—

fuel, environment, things that touch us profoundly, vividly, definitely. The media bombarded all of us with the need for this sacrifice and unselfishness.

I love America. I love Canada. So I prayed a lot to understand what it is that would make this thing successful, for at hand is the destruction of Planet Earth or its rebuilding. Many species of wild animals are going extinct because of our greed. Sacrifice is needed here, definitely. We were to look after the animals of the earth (Genesis 1:30) and not destroy them.

It seems almost useless to discuss pollution of the air we breathe and of the earth we work. Specialists have said that it will take years to rid the earth of all the harmful chemicals we have put into it for the sake of profit. The story goes on, of man's disobedience to God in tending the earth that God placed him on.

How long will we be able to live in the polluted air that we have created? How long can we live in our cities with the threat of violence, death, and tragedy?

In a word, we have sinned most thoroughly, and we have to atone; but we also know that the Lord understands and forgives our sin if we repent. So this is a call to repentance in the form of asceticism and penance. For this is the time of going back to the beginning, the beginning of the bible and of the gospel in particular. In the prophets we see fasting and prayer. Behind the fasting and prayer lies a deep abstinence from intellectual pride and from passions.

Feed the hungry, clothe the naked, visit the sick.

Asceticism is disciplining oneself for the sake of God and his law. But neither asceticism nor fasting nor penance mean a thing unless they are the fruit of love, which in itself comes from faith and hope. Unless each of us does pray and fast, the sacrifices that were asked for will never materialize, and our nation may continue for a while to think that we are masters of heaven and earth, instead of prostrating ourselves before God who is the master of all.

The poverty of the gospel burns like a fire in my soul. It seems to me that evangelical poverty is often discussed on a superficial level.

As Christians, we haven't dug deep enough into what poverty is all about.

The gospel requires what no political mandate would ever demand from its adherents. On a world scale, only an economy based on need and not on profit has any chance of succeeding. This requires sacrifice and renunciation. Living in a simple way might seem idiocy, but it will conquer. The essential principle is to be found in detachment in regard to all possessions.

The strange thing is that when you think you are totally detached, you discover an abyss of attachments. This hurts very much. How easily we are fooled. We will never know what poverty really is until we stop being avaricious, gluttonous, and preoccupied with ourselves.

The gospel says that if someone asks you for your cloak, give him your tunic, too. (Luke 6:29) We bicker about giving wheat to poor countries, about money needed for transportation of that wheat, when we ought to mortgage our houses, if need be, to help our neighbour. We walk in fear and we walk in guilt, because we're already before the judgment seat of God. Under the neon lights in our urban centers we toss and turn in our beds, unable to sleep in spite of all our pills. Why? Because deep down within us we know that we have not allowed Christ to live in our suburbs. We know that we have kept him out of jobs because he is African-American or Puerto Rican or of some other minority group.

Tranquilizers have ceased to tranquilize us because our consciences already stand before the all-seeing eye of God. We know we have too much to eat, too much to drink. We spend too much money on "good times," which turn out to be nightmares because the faces of the hungry people of the world haunt our bedrooms. Neither our soft background music nor our electric blankets pacify us because we dream of women giving birth to babies on dusty and filthy streets around the world. It is I who must feed the hungry, clothe the naked, visit the sick.

We are filled with guilt because the very means of communication we have invented are opening our eyes to the tragic mess that we, who think we are gods, have made of the world. We cannot sleep as peacefully as we did before, because the poverty of our brethren is brought into our living room on a small screen, piped in vividly and realistically. The inhuman life of many people today is a degrading sight; their condition defies description. Yet even the most degraded person is still a child of God and has his Spirit.

A wounded heart is a door for others to pass through to the heart of Christ.

Gospel poverty, however, is a way of life, our Christian calling. It is the fruit of the love of God, and the key to humility, which is truth. And since truth is God, poverty is a shortcut to God. We need to acknowledge our own intense personal poverty and realize that all we are, all we have, is from God.

Once you accept your own poverty before God and make it the very marrow of your thoughts, your life, your very being, you will become humble. You will walk in and with God. The acceptance of this truth will make you free, free to love and to serve in tragic circumstances. It will also make you free to love and serve God more passionately and constantly.

Gospel poverty moves into a totality of surrender of oneself, for no amount of giving pennies or dollars or millions of the same can take the place of that inner, deep, complete surrender. Then, comes the moment of saying, "Speak, Yahweh; for your servant is listening." (1 Samuel 3:10) This means one has turned from everything to God. At that moment, a lance penetrates one's heart. Then, your heart becomes a door through which a hundred, a thousand, a million people are led to God. Your wounded heart is a door for old feet, children's feet, middle age feet, anybody's feet to pass through to the heart of Christ. To have that kind of heart, that door-heart, is total poverty, in the gospel sense.

It is essential that our lives be a continual inner stripping of self. We may be called to let ourselves be stripped by others. First and foremost, this involves relinquishing our own wills and doing that of another. In this way, we can identify with the poor of the world and with Christ who was stripped for our sake. This will lead to our resurrection in him.

Chapter 4

The Church and Renewal

Anyone who wants to become great among you must be your servant, and anyone who wants to be first among you must be your slave, just as the Son of man came not to be served but to serve, and to give his life as a ransom for many.

Matthew 20:26-28

There is an immense cry for leadership in the Church today. We seem to be giving our children stones instead of bread. (Matthew 7:9) There is a great clamour for the Bread and Waters of Life, in the inarticulate cry of the multitudes. This drives me on, ever on, and yet who am I? Just an ordinary woman who sees and hears. But the burden of all this breaks my back, and my prayers are like tears that seem to fall on dry ground and be swallowed up. People's souls are being swallowed up by all the beasts of prey prowling around.

In certain Catholic circles, there is deep unrest regarding the structure of the Church. It seems that the word cannot be used any longer without negative connotations. Granted, structures need to be changed. But the process must be based on the folly of Christ and his cross, not on the sand of human intelligence and human wisdom. That means crucifixion, but also resurrection. If we build on any other foundation, what guarantee do we have that these new structures will be the right ones?

Probably because I am Russian, because I come from a different culture and background, and more probably because I have been reared on the scriptures, I see only one way of changing the structures of the Church—by remaining within the old structures until the Church accepts new ones, and then moving with the Church into new structures. While staying within the old structures, I humbly, truthfully raise my voice. I am not afraid of the consequences, even if it means crucifixion. I am immovable—like a tree standing by the living water flowing within the mystery of the Church. (Psalm 1:3)

During my years in the Lay Apostolate, I always lived within the structures of the Church, yet I also endured crucifixion and persecution. Only God knows what effect my life has had, but some of the structures have changed.

The dilemma felt by many Catholics is whether to flee from old structures in despair, or to stay within them, to die a thousand deaths, and to change them from within by love. We cannot stay on the periphery of the Church's life. From the surface, we will never come to understand the mystery of the Church. We need to enter into her tremendous, awesome mystery. We need to be the bride of the Christ. Christ will give us the love of his own heart if, in the darkness of faith, we enter into the essence of the Church's mystery.

We need to have a personal confrontation with God, and with his help solve our crises of faith.

The Church calls for conversion of every individual to the gospel of Jesus Christ, which is the deepest thing that the Christian can give to the secular world. What it hungers for most of all is God. The new catechetical methods, the new pastoral approaches, the new levels of involvement in the secular world and in our parishes will remain sterile without a personal confrontation with God.

We need to have a personal confrontation with God and, with his help, solve our crises of faith. It is in this realm that everything begins. Unless this personal dimension is straightened out, squarely faced, and lived by each Christian, nothing will really make sense.

Then the problem of authority will disappear, because Christians will become Christ's team. On a team, there is mutual respect and even reverence, since all work for the same goal and have the same motivation. Those engaged in specific ministries in the Church are called to take on the vision of the whole.

Until we are converted to the gospel of Jesus Christ, we will not obtain the tranquility of God's order but only the confusion of Babel. We cannot give the world anything it doesn't already have except God and God's love. But before we can give God to men, we need to be one with him ourselves. This kind of approach will be unchangeable until the *parousia*. There has never been a more effective program than to proclaim the gospel with one's life.

One does not arrive at all this rapidly or without effort. The journey leads to the liturgy, to the Eucharist, where alone we can find the grace and strength to become such lovers. To proclaim the gospel with our lives in a secular society, we need solitude, prayer, contemplation, and, especially, the Eucharistic sacrifice.

Enter into the pain of Christ and pray ceaselessly.

For people today, renewal involves a breaking up of the old and a rebuilding of the new. Both processes are painful to the soul, mind, and heart. This is a time for mutual charity. This is a time for building without destroying. To follow the spirit of the gospel is to deal gently and lovingly with things old and new. Let us help one another, humbly, prayerfully, lovingly. Let us go hand in hand toward the light and fire which the Holy Spirit has so lavishly poured upon us.

We must enter into the pain of Christ. Each of us needs to enter into the pain of Christ in order to bring the essence of his teaching into the world. We also need to enter into the prayer, the vigils, and the silence of Christ. There another encounter with him takes place. It is there, too, that the school of love teaches us patience—the martyrdom of love that we all need to undergo in order to become sparks in the wind of the Holy Spirit. Renewal will only take root in the world when it has taken root in us and when we have become rooted in Christ.

We want to follow in the footsteps of Christ and to have his rhythm. What did he do? He began his ministry by going into the desert. He preached to people he had been part of, as a carpenter, for many years. He also went into quiet places to pray. We cannot show our discipleship to Christ unless we love one another with his heart, which means we empty ourselves of that egotistical, selfish self that is like a high wall between us and God. Prayer alone can give us fortitude and courage to do that. The Apostle Paul told us to pray ceaselessly. (1 Thessalonians 5:17) It is through prayer and through eating the Bread and Wine—his Body—that we will achieve the betterment of society by coming to people with the love that every person seeks.

We are human. We are sinners. We are creatures of God. Let us each begin with ourselves. Let us see the beam in our own eye before we look for the mote in the eye of our neighbour. (Matthew 7:5)

We prove our love for God by loving our neighbour.

We may feel deeply concerned about all the tremendous needs of this tragic world of ours, about the poor and the social conditions in which so many injustices are visible, nationally and internationally. This concern is beautiful and as it ought to be, provided we have honestly and with pure hearts examined our relationship with those in our family and community, and kept our priorities straight.

However, many of us want to escape from facing ourselves in depth spiritually, or from facing God in depth, and to where do we escape? Naturally, into our work. There we have to meet people and things that demand immediate attention, and though we might be meeting them daily, we do not have to live with them as intimately as we have to live with ourselves and with others in our family or our community.

Although the gates of hell will not prevail against the Church, it could become just a handful of people hiding for their lives, when it should be a brilliant light on a mountain. We, the laity, have the power to send the Church into the catacombs again. Although we have an increase of charisms among the laity, with these comes an increase in grave responsibilities. In the tremendous mystery of the Church, we sinners and vessels of clay will either show the true face of Christ to a world which hungers for him, or we will blur that image.

To steer a clear course through the many shoals today, we need to be at peace and filled with wisdom from above. We need formation.

Formation of lay people is a simple channel through which flows the very breath of the Holy Spirit, reviving and revitalizing the Church.
It won't help to get too preoccupied with the human Church. There is a danger of breaking the vessels of clay and allowing the world-healing ointment of love to spill on the ground instead of on people's hearts. We cannot forget that on charity alone, love alone, we will be judged. We prove our love for God by loving our neighbour, the person next to us.

We need to get our priorities straight: seek first the kingdom of God.

Remember, bishops and the pope are our neighbours. It takes a very special type of courage these days to say a good word for the magisterium. The undercurrent of constant attack on them is disturbing. The pope, bishops, and priests often seem to be scapegoats.

Only when our hearts are full of love, will we be able to speak the truth with the gentle and healing voice of Christ who is Truth. He alone is without sin. He alone can take up the cords and chase the moneylenders out of the temple. (John 2:13–17) We dare not forget that to each one of us Christ addressed the words, "Let the one among you who is guiltless be the first to throw a stone." (John 8:7) Who among us is without sin and qualified to throw the first stones at the magisterium? Perhaps we ought to examine our own consciences. Perhaps before we criticize, we ought to repeat Christ's words to ourselves.

There are many, it is true, who really do attempt to begin with themselves, with the help of God's grace. It is they who are urged to take on the terrible burden of chaos and confusion in the souls of their brothers and sisters. Like Veronica offering Christ a cloth to wipe his face on the road to Calvary, they are called to stand by the Church in the face of lashes which seem to come directly from Satan.

The Church is in agony. The remedy is greater love, greater understanding, greater compassion, greater empathy for all who are confused, suffering, leaving the Church, tearing the seamless robe of Christ in the process.

The world has become a coliseum once again. Those who understand that true renewal begins with themselves will be handed over, as it were, to the beasts of hostilities and criticisms, confusion, denials, and apostasy. They will be ground into the invisible wheat of the bread of Christ. Having eaten of the God of love, they will be ready to be consumed themselves as holocausts and as martyrs. This invisible shedding of blood may be the seed of both a new faith and the finding of a lost one.

We, God's people, need to have our priorities straight. The gospel clearly states that the first concern of Christians is to seek the kingdom of God. (Matthew 6:33) It further states that once we have begun this search and have based our whole lives on this search, everything will be given to us. So it would seem that our first concern in updating the Church or changing society is to begin, not with the reformation of bishops or priests, but with ourselves. Are we really seeking the kingdom of God first?

The Church and every Christian is called to be prophetic.

The Christian and the whole Church is called to proclaim the glad news uncompromisingly, even if the world considers it bad news, disturbing news, unpleasant news. There can be no giving ground to any compromise with the message of the gospel. Christ said very clearly, "Anyone who is not with me is against me." (Matthew 12:30) Christ came to disturb the consciences of men. (John 16:7–11) He aroused people from their complacency, indifference, hedonism—stirred them to rise and follow him. The people who continue his mission are called to continue to disturb.

When I flinch in fear, I beg God to remind me that the cross is my heritage. We can neither conform to this world nor compromise with it. On the contrary, the Church and every Christian is called to be prophetic toward the world. Through our daily lives, we are to cry out loudly the word of God and be ready to be stoned, as were many of the prophets sent by the Lord.

The world is on the eve of tragedy and we have to be prepared for it. We need to examine the real priorities that face us today, the priorities of the Holy Spirit, and arrange our daily lives according to their demands.

It is essential that Christians first of all be totally one with Christ. Becoming one with Christ means undergoing inner conversion, a conversion that is beyond words to describe. Our God is a consuming fire, and we can enter into that fire, be cleansed, and catch fire ourselves. The Christian is to be totally with Christ, without any rationalization or compromise. For Christ, the resurrected Christ, the Lord of history, is the one who acts through the Christian upon the world. Only by being totally one with Christ, will the Christian be totally present to the world.

Among Christians today, there seem to be many who reject the Church or hurt her or push her around, and few devoted to her. We must always uphold the Church as obedient daughters and sons. True love never compromises, never conforms to anything which is not truth. A Christian is one who loves and who brings the message of love. We need to have courage to say what has to be said, even if what we say will not meet the approval of everybody at once. Ideas gel gradually in a group or community. Slowly an idea penetrates the mind and heart of another.

Christ said, "Here am I among you as one who serves!" (Luke 22:27) We, too, can "wash the feet" of others as Christ did and be ready to live out what he did and said. (Luke 22:27) This means serving in every possible way, political, economic, spiritual. Then, we will be a light to the feet of our brethren. If each one of us preaches the gospel with our lives, we stand out. It makes a difference to hundreds and thousands of people. Then they come to us to be strengthened and consoled and sometimes to be brought back to the arms of God and his Church.

Chapter 5

Community

*It is by your love for one another,
that everyone will recognize you as my disciples.*

John 13:35

How desperately we need Christian communities of love today. With God's help we can, even in our human frailty, form such communities, at various levels.

People who are drawn to the ideal of plunging into the Absolute, into God, should be the ones to form Christian community. They will become icons of Christ, that is, they will reflect Christ and make him available to people who no longer believe in mere words, to those who seek God's love through others.

Through the mutual love of the members, one for another, they will present the face of the living God, the resurrected Christ. He will so powerfully dwell in such families and communities that he will be touched and seen in those who call themselves his followers.

I live now, not I, but Christ lives in me.

Becoming a community means a total involvement in the other, and a total emptying of oneself so that each can say, "I live now, not I, but Christ lives in me." (Galatians 2:20) Then, the Christian community comes into existence. Then, like the Holy Spirit who truly formed it, a community becomes a fire burning in our midst, and from this fire sparks kindle the earth.

But no community can be established if we decide that we do not need the Trinity or Jesus Christ, or if we think that we can make our own god. Then, chaos reigns instead of community.

> There is a great need for alive Christian communities! The new ecclesial communities are the…providential response given by the Holy Spirit, to the critical challenge at the turn of the millennium.
>
> Pope John Paul II,
> 30 May 1998

Simply living in community brings one face to face with carrying the cross of others, for each person brings their pain, misery, and sorrows with them. God calls us to open our hearts to them, to all their fears and angers and unshed tears. We carry one another's crosses because Christ carried ours. God calls us to overcome our reluctance to leave the interior place we had become accustomed to and to come higher.

Prayer and love, love and prayer—these are children of faith and sisters of hope. They are the ingredients needed to form community. Nothing else will do.

Accept others as they are with grave humility, without trying to manipulate them.

The role of modern Christians is changing. This does not mean that we abandon the corporal works of mercy (to feed the hungry, give drink to the thirsty, shelter the homeless, care for the sick, visit the imprisoned, bury the dead). The poor will always remain with us. But our contemporary accent will be to show that Christ is alive, that the Holy Spirit is with us as he never was before, in a continual Pentecost. Where the Son is, there the Father is also. This can only be shown by the growth of love among us so that all the neo-pagans, all the atheists of today, will be compelled to say, "See how these Christians love one another."

This is the witnessing that we are called to do today. We can only do it by praying for an increase in faith, in courage, and in love. This is the hour of love and of loving. God is love. It is urgent that we bring him into the marketplace. The time is now.

On all sides, among all nations, peoples of all races and creeds are seeking answers not only to peaceful coexistence but to all their deepest needs of friendship and peace. Everywhere one sees a search for deeper communication and communion.

But the search will be in vain unless each one of us—each of us who forms part of a larger community of family, parish, town, city, nation—begins with a personal change of heart. For there can be no community, no peace, without a deep inner change of heart.

How does one change one's heart? It is impossible to change it by oneself, but it is possible through prayer. All other ways have failed. Let us pray to the Holy Spirit now, that he may help us change our hearts. The immediate future of mankind depends on this change of our hearts. Without the basis of a love which flowers into full acceptance of others, no peace can come to individual or nation.

To accept others as they are, without trying to manipulate them, is the beginning of establishing a family, a village, a nation. A community is based on love, a love that is all-embracing, that accepts the other with grave humility, no matter his race and creed or whether he be sick or healthy, ugly or beautiful, old or young.

Communities that have the love of God as their bond are the ones that endure.

Christian communities cannot be formed merely by a desire to join together, in order to be less lonely or more secure. Such motives cannot make a group of people into a community. Nor can communities be formed in a day.

A community is an organic reality which springs from being one in heart. There needs to be a cause, a reason which makes a group band together in the first place. And the reason must be greater than oneself, greater even than the good of the collective. Usually, the reason is spiritual. The Holy Spirit alone can hold people together. He alone can insure permanency. Communities that have the love of God as their bond are the ones that endure. The people in such communities realize that they come together, not for any ordinary reason (for example, to return to the land), but to incarnate in society Christ's law of love.

This means that such people were drawn, even before coming together, to a life of love, and hence to the service of God and their neighbour. They come ready for discipline, a personal discipline, which is absolutely necessary for living with a group of people.

Actually, communities of this sort are made up of very "foolish" people, for the wisdom of God is foolishness to us. (Matthew 11:25)

Seek not to be loved, but to love.

Let us review what it means to be a member of a Christian community. Here I speak of community not in the sense of a city, village, or even parish, but of smaller groups who come to live a common life together, out of love for God and others.

First and foremost, members of this community are called to love God with a totality that is absolute, always tending in faith toward that absolute throughout their lives. Entry into such a community means to become a pilgrim of the Absolute, to be absolutely dedicated to this ideal.

Secondly, it means loving your neighbour as yourself. Here is the catch—before you can become a dedicated member of any community, you need to love yourself. Love yourself by accepting yourself as you are, by stopping the manipulation of others. It means a constant effort toward achieving gospel poverty and purity of heart, and embracing the ideals of St. Francis: "not seeking to be consoled but to console; not to be loved, but to love." This is what is meant, in part, by loving oneself. There is more, but the rest will come slowly from the Holy Spirit. When one begins to love oneself, one can begin loving one's neighbour.

Even more than incarnating the words of St. Francis, we need to incarnate the words of God himself. Christ said, "It is by your love for one another, that everyone will recognize you as my disciples." (John 13:35) Obviously, this is impossible. For who of us can love with the heart of God? We cannot. But we can enter into the immense travail of emptying our hearts of everything that impedes the coming of the Lord. As this happens, the community begins to be cemented together by love. Now it grows strong, having grown organically, and having recognized that its growth is contingent on God's law of love.

But it must go further. Each member is called to love those who hurt or seemingly hate him or her. Here the foolishness of the cross bites deeply. For above all they are called to love any member of their community who is hurtful to them, who seems to hate them.

This, like the emptying, the *kenosis*, will require prayer. The members of any community of the type we are treating here need to be people of deep prayer. In fact, constant prayer. (1 Thessalonians 5:17) Without prayer the law of the love of God cannot be incarnated. Each needs to be prepared to fulfill Christ's last commandment of love: "No one can have greater love than to lay down his life for his friends." (John 15:13)

Joyfully surrender.

Secularism can make inroads into a Christian family or community through a subtle relaxation of cherished and sacred principles. For example, this is reflected in comments about not liking the job we are given to do or the place we are assigned to, a kind of nattering, an illusive negative reaction. An illusive thing can break up a family, a community, a nation.

We are called to joyfully surrender our likes and dislikes, our talents if need be, our whole person to the need of our family or community, since it is God who has brought us together.

A Christian community can be based only on God and his incredible, immense, wondrous law of love. It is this love which is the need of the times. Nothing else will do.

Love as Christ loves us, love with Christ's heart, love with a total surrender to God in the other.

I was asked to speak to a group of religious concerning "forming a community of love." What I had to say was simple and pertained to what I consider the essence of things. That essence is summed up in St. Paul's beautiful hymn of charity: "Love is always patient and kind; love is never jealous; love is not boastful or conceited, it is never rude and never seeks its own advantage, it does not take offence or store up grievances. Love does not rejoice at wrongdoing, but finds joy in the truth. It is always ready to make allowances, to trust, to hope, and to endure whatever comes." (1 Corinthians 13:4–7)

No matter how long or how many times I meditate on that passage, I am awed by it. God seems to ask the impossible. We who are called his disciples, his followers, are asked to love one another with his heart. How can an ordinary person love with the heart of God?

Nevertheless, this kind of love is the essence, the cornerstone, the foundation; it is the answer to all the questioning, confusion, turmoil, and unrest which are presently shaking us. First, foremost, and last, before we talk about our services to others, we need to ask ourselves: Have we begun to love the people in the community in which God has placed us? It may be a family, a lay apostolic community, a religious community, the parish, a village, a neighbourhood. Have we begun to love the people with whom we live?

Communication must lead to communion. Before I can communicate lovingly with anybody, I have to be in communion with that person. Communion is a form of love. Do I really love? Do I really believe?

Unless we start with the conviction that we shall be recognized as Christ's disciples only through loving as he loved us, all will be chaff in the wind. The most profound dialogue is between two crucified people.

Training comes through persons who live what Christ taught.

Christians, especially youth, are desperately trying to get in touch with God in one way or another. All kinds of programs and courses are being set up to teach theology, scripture, and catechetics.

I am often asked what kind of program, course, or other kind of training I consider to be needed in our days, and how we train people in our apostolic community of Madonna House. Strangely enough, I am hesitant. The answers do not seem to come easily. I was brought up in the Russian tradition, which emphasizes normal, human, family relationships. The "gurus" were parents or teachers or someone in charge of the very young.

I don't know if these people could be called charismatic or not. They simply had the tradition of Christianity at work in them—a love of the Trinity, a deep understanding of the role of the Holy Spirit in our life, a living understanding of the scriptures, and participation in the Divine Liturgy, as Russians call the Mass.

Real training and formation came from someone who lived what Christ taught, or tried to live it. That someone was a person who had made contact with God through prayer and action.

No wonder Thomas Merton found his way to the East in order to discover how the guru was able to reach down and get into the depths of a disciple. It is often difficult for the Western mind to comprehend the guru-disciple relationship. It exists in Russia, too, for Russia is part of the East, and a very important part. Russia, in many ways, has absorbed much of Eastern wisdom. The guru-disciple relationship was the way the Master himself taught.

I have to hesitate when questions of training are posed to me. I hesitate even more when people ask about contacting God. "How do I meet Christ?" people ask.

I have found no shortcuts in meeting Christ. I have found him in the humble daily routine of human existence. Perhaps it began with my mother and my father, but especially my mother, who easily and simply made connections between the daily life of a little girl as she grew up and God. This was my tradition—all things are related to God, and one can find God in them.

Perhaps this is why I find it difficult to outline in any logical, intellectual way my answer to those who ask what training should be. I feel like crying out that it is all so clear. The training we need to give is the training Christ gave his apostles, and which the apostles gave the early Christians, the training that made them capable of going to the arenas of the pagan world, the training that eventually made slave and master one in the same household.

I think contemporary youth understands my hesitation. They, too, seek the guru-disciple relationship. Their search for God is increasing. They are truly hastening to find the Lord.

It is obvious, too, that the Holy Spirit is indeed training us today. The "Seat of Wisdom" is making us wise without many courses, just to show us that one can meet God in the Mass, in the Word of God, in following Christ from Nazareth to Calvary. Wisdom means to be folded in the wings of the Crimson Dove, as the Russians call the Holy Spirit. These are the answers I would give to questions of formation.

It seems that my theme song is the same no matter where I am asked to speak—we are called to love one another as Christ loved us, in whatever community he has placed us. We are asked to love one another with Christ's own heart, with a total surrender to God in the other. To form such a community of love means accepting the cross, carrying it, and being crucified on it. (Luke 9:23–25) Only then can we live in the resurrected Christ. (Romans 6:3–7) Wherever there is love there is pain, sometimes a terrible pain that tears us apart—but only so that God can put us back together again.

Such is the essence of forming a community, and we need to begin with this essence or we will fail. Since we are human and cannot accomplish this of ourselves, we are compelled to make contact with God through whom, by whom, and in whom alone we can achieve this miracle of love. Prayer, therefore, is also of the essence—the prayer of the Eucharist, and the constant prayer of the heart, the prayer of silence. All such prayer will lead us unerringly to the essence.

Chapter 6

Modern Society

> I was hungry and you gave me food,
> I was thirsty and you gave me drink,
> I was a stranger and you made me welcome,
> lacking clothes you clothed me,
> sick and you visited me,
> in prison and you came to see me....
> In so far as you did this to one of the least of these brothers of mine,
> you did it to me.
>
> Matthew 25:35-36, 40

Our technological miracles have brought in their wake fears that we never knew before. We have nightmares of becoming robots and mere extensions of machines. We feel dehumanized by economic and political situations.

We Christians can respond to a depersonalized society by being intensely personal, and by basing our lives on love. For depersonalization leads to utter loneliness, and we Christians hold within our heart and soul a solution—personal relationships. In this apocalyptic age, we can offer love.

It is important that we talk with others about our relationship with God, and his with us. We are called to reveal to others our relationship with God, and his with us. It is urgent that we allow people to touch God through sharing with them our relationship with him. We need to take our strength from Christ and be open with others.

If your world seems de-personalized, then put your person into it and make it personalized.

Today people are excited and enamored of any new technology that will help us escape from reality, that will help us speed to some "better place." Actually, we go nowhere, only to return to where we started.

Although technological communication through satellite promises to make us one world, more and more persons have become islands. Many technological advancements and gadgets only fragment us further.

Nations, too, can become islands. Then, war and violence break out and lead to an ultimate chaos.

Technology is bringing us a million changes a minute, one might say. Without a change of heart we may be able to make use of the benefits of technology, but we will also abuse them, to the detriment of the common good—abuse them even unto the destruction of one another. In all of this, religion and ethics and even normal behaviours disappear or are ridiculed.

The words of President Kennedy echo in my ears, "Ask not what your country can do for you, but what you can do for your country." These memorable words can be applied to many things besides countries.

If my work or living place seems de-personalized, then let me put my person into it and make it personalized so that each person cares for the other. Let us be alert that no one is overlooked. If the place seems too big or too technological, it is up to each one of us to make it livable by paying attention to each other, by friendship with each person, by a hundred ways in which a person can reduce bigness to an atmosphere of

> *The sacredness of the human person cannot be obliterated, no matter how often it is devalued and violated, because it has its unshakable foundation in God as Creator and Father.*
>
> Pope John Paul II
> *Vocation and Mission of the Lay Faithful*

warmth and simplicity. It is up to each one of us. In a word, "Not what my country can do for me, but what I can do for my country."

God loves us, not because we are good but because he is good.

Contemporary persons suffer from the inability of seeing themselves as they are, because their idea of their personality is formed predominantly by seeing their reflection in the eyes of others. Because of the breakdown in family life, most people have not known the love that is the food of personality development. This begets a nonacceptance of self.

Today it is not a personal privilege or misfortune to be neurotic or emotionally wounded. Millions and probably billions of people are wounded, due to the tremendous surge of history in the past century with its rapid technological changes, wars, uprootedness, and insecurity.

One of the greatest tragedies of our times is the loss of our identity, especially among the young. It is a loss of identity that seems to be accompanied by an inability to love and accept oneself. Youth reject themselves and, thus, alienate themselves from God and from their neighbours.

People are fragmented beings, today. Contemporary persons are divided within themselves. We are insecure, with hot and cold wars, and threats of nuclear war hanging overhead. A partial cause of this fragmentation, of this division within oneself, is our rejection of all the ways of old, of much of the wisdom of the past. Frightened and impatient, we want to shake off all shackles that seem to bind us. Any kind of authority appears to us as a shackle which impedes our free movements.

What is to be done about this situation?

We have recourse to psychiatry and psychology to put ourselves back together again. But all they do is perhaps give us some insight into ourselves and our emotional patterns. Then, they ask us to use our own resources to make ourselves whole. But we can't. We need more than science. We need God. If we would arise and go in search of God, we would find the wholeness we seek. The Lord will not leave us alone, shepherdless, Fatherless.

Much of our fragmentation could be healed if we followed the advice of the Book of Proverbs. That is, if each generation preserved the wisdom of the past, added to it prayer, fasting, and living truthfully, and then passed this treasure on to its children, there would always be a harmonious blending of the old with the new.

We need the wisdom of God much more than that of science and psychiatry. God's wisdom would lead us to wholeness even in our nuclear age. We need to put away our desire for childishness. It is essential that we stop being fools who desire what is harmful for ourselves. We must cease to hate true knowledge, true wisdom, which is God himself, and begin earnestly to search for it. We need to become childlike in order to be fully mature, grown-up, and responsible people.

The answer is to preach the gospel with one's life. The gospel can be summed up in the two commandments of love: Love God and love your neighbour as yourself. (Matthew 22:37–39) Christians, young, old, and in between need to understand that one can love neither God nor one's neighbour unless one loves oneself and accepts oneself as being unique, irreplaceable, beloved by the God who created us. God loves us, not because we are good, but because he is good.

Show God's love to those who feel unlovable.

The restoration of the world begins with each one of us, person by person. It would be foolish to try to restore the world *en masse*. We begin and continue to restore it person by person, beginning with ourselves. For the gospel of love and of faith that liberates humanity is preached and witnessed to by one person to another. It cannot be otherwise given. It's a person to person relation.

Let there arise among us people who, falling in love with God, will show God's love to anyone who feels unlovable and cannot accept himself. If all those who suffer from an identity crisis could see Christ's love shine in the eyes of a Christian, they would be healed. Love would be let loose in the world. Christ would become visible again.

Every Christian is called to become a person restored in Christ.

Developing the true personality of persons is a gigantic task.

Our life experiences not only form us but can add to our stature as a person if we appraise their inner essence. Our sickness and pain, our humiliations and failures, the monotonous aspects of our lives, all give us profitable experiences. They enlarge our vision of life. We can appraise the inner essence of every experience. It has long been the urge of my heart to restore people to total wholeness.

Most of us can be healed and restored by the simple process of being loved, together with knowledge acquired through study or counselling. A warm family or community life, learning manual labour skills and crafts, academic training or study, especially scriptural and liturgical, and travel—all of these help to liberate one's personality and bring it towards its full potential.

In our community, I developed many different departments, from cooking to carpentry to office to gardening to library to cleaning to automotive repair, to arts and crafts. By working in each area, a person becomes more whole, more confident, less fragmented. For example, by restoring broken things, by recycling what people throw away, one grows in maturity, for the Lord did say to gather up the fragments lest they be lost. (John 6:12) One learns a lot through dealing with them; one sees that out of what was "one person's scrap" comes "another person's gold."

Fostering growth of the whole person, of one's personhood, involves restoring the intellect and creativity, and emotional and volitional restoration, as well as manual labor skills, which give a foundation for everything else. Learning a sense of stewardship and constant self discipline in the area of living a gospel poverty, also contributes to the growth of the spirit and to a developed person.

Every Christian is called to become a person restored in Christ and needs to have the benefit of the whole gamut of intellectual, cultural, and spiritual resources necessary for this. The study of the spiritual life or of spiritual things is the crown of all knowledge.

To obey is to love, to govern is to love.

Jesus Christ, the most mature human being that ever lived, stressed obedience to his Father. God speaks of himself as Father. And Jesus said that he came to do the will of his Father. (John 5:30) He was obedient even unto death on a cross.

Why is it that today we rebel against this very essence of Christ's teaching? All authority seems vested in the father figure. The understanding of authority stems from father and mother figures. But there is a wholesale rebellion against those figures. Why did Christ take a little child (the child in ourselves that we fight against, the child that we do not want to be) and say, "Unless you change and become like little children you will never enter the kingdom of heaven"? (Matthew 18:3)

Gospel obedience can only be based on love and be given freely. In the gospel sense, to obey is to love, just as to govern is to love. Authority exists to serve.

Service and love and trust are the basis of authority, which comes from Christ. He told us that he "came not to be served but to serve." (Matthew 20:28) We need to remember that God has chosen those in authority and he knew their weaknesses. Since he bears with them in his mercy, can we not also bear with them in our mercy? Our obedience needs to be given with a full and mature realization as to why it is given.

The essence of life is to be with God in our hearts all the time.

Restoring the world to Christ via living the gospel means doing little things with great love for God and for neighbour. This restoration, this proclaiming of the gospel through one's life is factually one of the most powerful means of renewing the Church.

This is factually done person to person, even in mass communications and through mass media. There it can be girded to the individual receiving the message, because between the giving of the message and the receiving of it, the Holy Spirit enters. Each person is unique and irreplaceable and will get out of the message what the Holy Spirit will help them to get.

It stands to reason that the apostle needs to be ready, needs to be restored himself or herself, before being able to give the renewing message to others. Some, of course, need more restoration than others, but in our apostolic community we see the miracle of complete or almost complete restoration of persons. It is a slow process, because it is thorough and constantly deals with the mystery of grace. Haste, unpreparedness, and lack of formation—spiritual, intellectual, creative, physical, and so on—is a tragedy. We need patience, which is the first definition of charity in St. Paul's hymn. (1 Corinthians 13:4–7) Yet, we may not be sluggish in our efforts.

The individual person is so important because it is through one person that another is reached, by God's grace. Through individual persons the Church becomes the sign of love to the world.

It is urgent that we develop communities of love, where the atmosphere is conducive to losing the insecurity and feelings of inadequacy, of fears and hostility, that form the wounds of contemporary persons. We need to help each other.

Let us especially pay attention to our own. There are so many lonely people amongst us. Let us drop the barriers of fear and rejection, cross the divide, and offer ourselves to others in our own family. Let us go to them and reduce their loneliness with the warmth of our faith, our hope, and our love. Only then can we console the rest of the world. Listen to God pleading within your heart.

Hospitality of the heart means accepting others as they are.

What the world needs most today is hospitality of the heart. Hospitality of the heart means accepting all others as they are, allowing them to make themselves at home in one's heart. To be at home in another person's heart means touching love, the love of a brother and sister in Christ. Touching the love of another means realizing that God loves us. For it is through the other—our neighbour, our brother—that we can begin to understand the love of God.

This is especially necessary in our strange technological loneliness that has separated us so thoroughly, not only from our neighbours, but from our fathers, mothers, grandparents—in short, from our relations. Our technological age has begotten a terrible loneliness.

We are called to give the hospitality of the heart. In other words, we are asked to open ourselves to a sharing of friendship that is rooted in the very heart of Christ whom we call our friend.

Hospitality of the heart is an answer to people's hunger for God. Through our hospitality they will know love, care, gentleness, understanding, listening. As Christ said, "You visited me...you came to see me." (Matthew 25:35–36)

Take notice of each person you meet.

People today are crying out for recognition. They want to be seen as a person among other persons. People want to be noticed, not in any ostentatious way, not because they might or might not have money, but just because they are a human being, a person. The greatest need of all is the need to be loved.

But we pass by one another without noticing, without stopping, without the slightest sign of recognition. This is why people daily come closer to despair, and why they frantically continue to search for the one who will love them.

It is time that Christians began to take notice of each person they meet. Each person is a brother or sister in Christ. Each person needs to be recognized, to be given a token of friendship and love, be it only a smile, a nod of the head. Sometimes it may require the total availability of one person to another if they are to fill a particular person's hunger for God. Such love and recognition must always be given with deep reverence, irrespective of the status of the person encountered.

There is something in each of us that has dignity. I've worked with every kind of person in my life, not only the prostitute, but murderers and thieves. In each, I found beauty, and I stood utterly helpless before the wounds inflicted by life.

All of us have the same terrible needs as they—the desire to be loved and accepted, and not sentimentally. Speaking for myself, persecution can take away one's dignity. We have to face each other with immense gentleness, and we need to respect that strange thing we call integrity. It is essential that we treat men and women not as things but as persons, and that we not manipulate them.

We have to be very careful with each other, for each has wounds given from childhood by parents, our environment, our teachers, or whomever. We often use salt to keep those wounds open in one way or another. Let our charity not be sentimental. Let us treat people with integrity and let us listen, listen and pray. It is only through listening and prayer that we will understand the hurt of the other, that you will understand my hurt and I will understand yours. Let us treat each person with deep integrity and respect and let us console, for through us flows the love of God the Father, the grace of the Son, and the illumination of the Holy Spirit.

We who have been projected into the atheism of our century have to confront a terrifying loneliness. With all the technology at our disposal from TV and radio to computers and various gadgets of telephoning, contemporary people walk alone.

Yet God created us to be friends with one another, and friends with him, to have a dialogue with each other and to have a dialogue with him. We can listen to one another and to God because God is in us.

We Christians are called to have a listening heart, a heart that takes in the whole world, persons of all races and creeds. A listening heart has a quality of listening with one ear to the person in our presence and the other ear to God.

But it takes quite a while for these listening ears to realize that it is by means of Christ's death that we receive the ability to listen with one ear to a brother or sister and the other ear to God. When we do, God renews our hearts, through our faith.

The grip of loneliness can be broken.

While it is true that the gospel requires us to share our physical goods, and many of us do, or try to, we have somehow often forgotten that human beings do not live by bread alone. (Matthew 4:4) It is this very dimension of love that we are reluctant to give our neighbour.

Loneliness holds the people of our age and times in a grip that seems unbreakable. Yet it can be broken. It can be broken by love, a love offered silently and gently from one human heart to another. It may be a love expressed in words, words that come from a heart united with God in the quiet prayer of contemplation. It is not enough for Christians to simply love. We are called to love with the very heart of Christ himself.

In order to do so, we need to open our hearts to humanity. We are asked to take upon ourselves the pain of each person as Christ did. We are called to identify ourselves constantly with the lonely ones and to share their loneliness. It is essential that we die to self. Then, Christ will live in us and love in us. In the face of such love, loneliness will depart and our world will be able to gather itself together. The islands will merge into a mainland, the one body of Christ.

Reverence, understanding, and hospitality of the heart—these are the immediate, intense needs of persons today. Are we Christians going to wake up and act as Christians, incarnating the law of love into our daily lives in real depth? Or are we going to compromise and allow people to continue to plunge into their dark nights looking for someone who will say to them, "My brother, I am here. Come. I have water and a towel. Sit down. Let me wash your tired feet that have pilgrimaged for so long. I recognize you as my brother. I revere you. I love you." These meetings are the true crossroads of time and history.

Loneliness has a door and we, each one of us, have the key to it. The key is acceptance of the other, without questions. Acceptance makes the other realize that he or she is loved, and because we have given them our love we can now give them the fruit of love—tenderness, compassion, gentleness, and understanding.

Yes, I have the key to the loneliness of the other, and the other has the key to my loneliness. The only thing we have to do is insert it into the keyhole of our hearts, open the door, and enter. But we are afraid, because this means a deep, loving involvement with the other. We prefer to be involved in some project or place of our own choosing where we don't have to use a key to one another's heart.

Give the alms of loving, gentle, thoughtful words.

The Word was made flesh and dwelt among us. (John 1:14) The uncreated God became man, for love of us. The Word of God walks among us and yet millions know him not (John 1:10) in our dark and fearsome days. Yet the fate of our world and its civilization depends upon our knowing him and loving him. It is time that we, the children of his light and love, make him known.

Many are the ways we can do this. None is simpler, more direct, than through almsgiving. Not only of gold and silver, for some may not have any. Not only of food or clothing, since not all may have a surplus to give or know where to seek those in need. But all of us can give the alms of words, which are needed by all at some time, and by many at all times. They can be given at any time and everywhere. They are needed everywhere.

Like all other alms, words need to be given lovingly, gently, thoughtfully. To be able to dispense the alms of words, one has to be one with The Word, our Lord Jesus Christ, to be on the way toward dying to self and living in him. One needs to see with his gentle eyes, think with his mind, love with his burning heart—or at least endeavour to.

Alms given without love, without compassion or gracious pity or deep understanding, bring hurt and pain. Somehow they prostitute the very act of giving. But when, watchful and alert in the cause of Christ, we see our neighbours as he would see them, love will give us understanding and allow us to read the signs of hungry minds, numbed hearts, frightened and lonely souls, and broken bodies. Going even deeper, we may hear symphonies of pain and hurt, fear, and near despair that life and the Prince of Evil play on the strings of emotions, with endless variations.

Everywhere and anywhere the ministry of love, of giving the alms of our words, can be exercised. Take the other person into your heart. In so doing, you take Christ into your heart, and surely he will reverse the process in eternity—he will take you into his heart.

Do our eyes really see? Are we not blind to the thousands of little things that exist in our own family? Father is a little grayer, a little more worried, a bit more silent. Mother is more tense, often with eyes that speak of tears shed in hiding. Sister or brother speaks more sharply, less pleasantly, or is more withdrawn. These may indicate the beginning of tragedies.

Is our love watchful, vigilant, ready to give the alms of gentle words spoken in time, key words that may open a closing door? A gate may be opened, allowing light and love to flood the depths of minds that are beginning to doubt love's very existence.

Are we sold on being our brother's keeper? Do we understand how far and how deep this "keeping" goes? Business associates, friends, fellow workers, strangers who cross our paths, the whole of our daily workaday world—all are our "brothers" whom we are asked to cherish in the Lord. (Matthew 25:35–40)

A smile and maybe a word about the weather given to an ill-clad poor person in a public conveyance, or to an immigrant from a distant culture, may mean the difference between his hatred of all we stand for and all God is, and the opposite. Clearly enunciated words, spoken slowly and lovingly with a smile of encouragement are rich alms given foreigners who are still shy with our language. Here again the alms of our words can change the fate of our nation.

We need to be alert that our speech not show an unconscious superiority, especially in the presence of persons from minority groups. For this stammering, shy alien who barely speaks English may tomorrow become the leader of hate and revolt, and may do untold damage to minds, souls, and bodies. And all because no one took time to give the alms of gentle, understanding words when these were food and drink to a thirsty and hungry stranger.

The sick may be tiresome at times in their self-centeredness, in their urgency to take us through every step of their domain of loneliness and pain, via their halting, rambling, repetitious speech. How are we to console them, bring them back to the realms of God's light and love? We can show them that their sufferings are a treasure that can save worlds of souls everywhere if only they offer that loneliness and those pains to Mary, the treasurer of God, his Mother. How else but through the alms of our comforting words, our patient, interested, unflagging care, can they learn the importance of offering her their goods?

The forgotten, the unwanted, the lost, the rambling alcoholic, the neurotic, the borderline "psychos"—would they be what they are if someone had given them the alms of words when these were so desperately needed? Words of love, understanding, compassion, patience, help, are to them oils that soothe burning wounds of exhausted minds. They are food that nourishes a starvation resembling that found in concentration camps. Words are often, to them, keys that open prison doors. They are so easy to give, yet so often withheld.

To the elderly, the unwanted, with their senile ramblings, their childishness, their tempers, and their hungry loneliness, alms of kind warm words are like a mother's lullaby, bringing peace and joy into joylessness and unpeace, making them feel wanted and loved again.

The pariahs of our modern world, the "bums," pan-handlers, prostitutes, prison inmates, what about them? Who has the time and courage to give them the alms of words, or the courtesy of an attentive silence?

Everywhere people silently cry out for the alms of words, for they are thirsty for love and friendship. Let us open the doors of our hearts now, before they are frozen shut by some new technological achievement. The choice is clear—either we love with the heart of Christ, or we die a strange death of being lifeless robots. God is love. God is the Word. He clothed himself in flesh for love of us. Let us then show him to our brothers, especially through the alms of loving words.

A production mentality blinds us to our true worth: the life and death of Christ, our redeemer.

Our civilization judges people by their conformity to existing superficial standards—by what they produce. We often cannot accept ourselves because of this yardstick, because we measure ourselves by our ability to produce, by our "production quotient." We think we are only worth what we can produce. Our society, culture, mores all seem to gang up on us from childhood to make us believe in this yardstick.

We measure ourselves as if we were extensions of machines instead of machines being an extension of ourselves. Salaries are raised in the business world according to our production: How many items have we sold? How many orders have we brought in? What were our grades in class? How many insurance policies did we sell? And so on.

With the all-pervading cultural pattern of North America in the background, we need to look at the gospel. In this cultural environment, there is a tremendous conflict between the production mentality and the essence of things. The essence may be said to be the gospel about serving two masters, God or mammon, (Matthew 6:24) and the gospel about the lilies of the field and the birds of the air. (Matthew 6:25–34)

We seek the kingdom of God first within our souls, and when the noise from within or without becomes unbearable, we need not hesitate to stop and drop everything and go to a private place and pray. We would retire from action if we had the flu. How much more so for God! This is not an easy hurdle for people in this culture who feel guilty for not working.

Failures are thought reprehensible. But without failures there can be no successes. Failures are stepping-stones to success, even in the natural order of things. True, they may cause a devastating loss of face. But with God every moment is the moment of beginning again.

The Lord can make successes out of failures. Our job is only to sow, his is the harvest. Let us face our failures head on, for time and failure are married to each other and through perseverance can produce beauty and joy. The essence is to be present before God in our hearts all the time. We look to Christ's life for our model.

The production mentality blinds us to our true value. The incarnation, death, and resurrection of Christ are the real measure of our true value. We are worth three hours of his agony on the cross. More, we are worth Jesus' whole life. For the Father so loved the world that he gave his only Son. (John 3:16) This is our worth.

Chapter 7

Christian Culture

Blessed are the pure in heart: they shall see God.

Matthew 5:8

In these high-tech, secular times it is important that we continue to develop and preserve Christian culture, which reflects the impenetration of God through love into all parts of human life. Each family, each community, is called to create a Christian climate in our homes. Our love for God must permeate our whole life. Christian culture expresses our faith and helps to transmit it to the next generations.

We are meant to attain the fullness of our humanity. We are to become a truly Christian civilization, for our humanity is penetrated through and through by the presence of Christ. All of reality around us is to be penetrated by Christ. In each family and Christian community, we are to be a city of God upon earth, a place where the human and the Christian blend, where Christ is incarnated in the human.

Our society is increasingly secular, depersonalized and dehumanized. In many instances the relationship is more to a machine than to people. The relationship is with TV, computer, with machines of one type or another, and interpersonal relationships are thus diminished. In our person and as a family, we can be a refuge against the dehumanization of the world.

Our relationships are person to person. Our relationship to work is a human one. Our environment needs to have cultivated everything that is human—poetry, dancing, singing, painting, drama, hospitality, helping the poor, all the arts. Not just work. It is easy to fall into a concept of life as work, pray, eat, sleep. But it is more than that. We are meant to have a full, total life. A life where Christian culture is developed.

A powerful image of this comes to mind from my Russian background, an image known as the protected city of Novgorod. Located near the city of Petrograd on the Dnieper River in Russia, it was a great trade and cultural center during the Middle Ages. When the Tartars invaded Russia in the thirteenth century they were unable to penetrate into the region of Novgorod because of the forest which made fighting much more difficult. The Russians in that area were accustomed to forest fighting, a guerrilla type of warfare, so the Tartars didn't move into that area. As a result, Novgorod was left free to develop.

Only from within and through culture does the Christian faith become a part of history and the creator of history.

Pope John Paul II,
Vocation and Mission of the Lay Faithful

What developed there was a Christian Russian culture. So much so that after the Tartars left, the geniuses and saints and artists of Novgorod spread throughout Russia and became the foundation of the renewal of Russian Christian life. So the image of Novgorod is that of a protected city which not only preserves but develops faith and culture so that when freedom comes it can be shared with other people.

Artists are God's troubadours of beauty.

Artists are God's troubadours of beauty. Art includes not only painting, sculpting, ceramics, weaving, and the like, but also drama and music and writing, everything and anything that is creative. When one has received the gift of creating, it is never for oneself and one's own satisfaction.

Beauty is God-related. We are called to bring his many-faceted beauty to the world. He wants his beauty to be presented with love, so that it shows the face of God, in whatever form it may be presented. Love and peace can be the frames of whatever we produce; they need to come from the very depths of the artist's soul. Then when we deal in beauty, love will grow out of it, hope will shine from it, and faith catch the heart of the beholder.

Just as Novgorod was protected by the trees, so we have to make sure that our "forest" grows thicker and thicker—the forest of our faith, our hope, our love, so that it cannot be penetrated and destroyed.

God constantly restores us, constantly makes us new. There is a loneliness that comes from God so that we may awaken to the power within us, to our neglected ability to make things new or to create beauty out of something. This is a loneliness of faith, a creative loneliness, one that makes us bring beauty and new life to others.

A Christian artist is a disturber of people, in the sense that Christ was.

Art, beauty, and creativeness liberate the spirit and bring peace. Creativity is one of the five needs of human beings—finding beautiful, creative ways to fill the daily needs of clothing, housing, tools, foods, and entertainment. We have a need to bring beauty into our surroundings. Even junk can be made into beauty and waste can be restored to usefulness.

It is essential that Christian artists be humble people, for humility means living in truth, and an artist is called to live in truth with God, with himself, and with the world. What form this truth is given depends on the individual artist, but whatever it is, it must give the Word, whether in ceramics, painting, carving, or any other art medium. It need not be religious art, because their work is to remind people that God is the creator. But the artist is called to be a person of prayer, silence, joy, and peace, notwithstanding the artistic tensions inherent in his or her creating.

Christian artists are called to express love, and beauty—as they understand it. They will see it through Christ, who is humility, truth, beauty, the Way, the Word, but each will see it as the facet of a diamond, for many facets bring forth the beauty of the whole.

A Christian artist is also a disturber of people, in the sense that Christ was. He does not allow them to fall into mediocrity. An artist is a person in love with God and humanity; he is a bridge between the two.

Christian artists need to be people of great mercy and compassion, tolerance and understanding. These go with humility, for, living in truth, they will know that beauty is in the eye of the beholder. They don't look down from the height of their technical training, art appreciation, or personal artistic insight on the artistic choices of other persons. At the same time, they have a duty to teach others, in a gentle and tender way, and to lead people to other, more beautiful art forms and art appreciation. I did this constantly in our community, displaying examples of different qualities of art, side by side. Christian artists know they are creatures, know that they have to lean on God. They know that God is the great artist.

We are God's work of art, created in Christ Jesus for the good works which God has already designated to make up our way of life.

Ephesians 2:10

Intellectuals and experts are also called to be humble, poor, simple and childlike, and to use their competence to serve people.

Christian culture includes intellectual works in the various fields of science and theology. These experts, too, are called to be humble, poor, simple, and childlike, and to use their talents and competencies as tools of service for all people. We have one aim: that people know God, know that he loves them, and that they love him back, that they see him in eternity. This is the greatest good that I can wish for my neighbour. Love commands the eternal search to bring that knowledge to your fellow man, in every possible discipline. All sociology, all politics, must be subservient to the primary good of reaching eternal life.

We have to be sensitive, sensitive of heart.

Culture is an intangible thing and includes listening with the heart. Because of the gospel we adopt other people's cultural patterns when we enter their sphere of living. We try to follow the cultural pattern of wherever we are, with courtesy, according to the mores of the country.

We have to be sensitive, sensitive of heart. But in order to be sensitive of heart, we have to be sensitive with the five senses, we have to develop them. Then we become more cultured. Culture is the ability to see the other person's point of view, to blend with them, to develop a living civilization. Exposure to culture through our senses brings increased sensitivity of soul, heart, and mind.

We are each commissioned by God to bring the holy originality, holy individuality, that he created in us to a world that is becoming robot-like in its conformity. Let us be adventuresome in our creative outlets and in our prayers and our sanctity, and share the wealth of our efforts. Let us not be afraid to think and to seek answers to our questions. Let us not be afraid to be different.

Your light must shine in people's sight, so that, seeing your good works, they may give praise to your Father in heaven.

Matthew 5:16

Chapter 8

My Brother's Keeper

> Jesus began his proclamation with the message,
> "Repent for the kingdom of Heaven is close at hand."
>
> Matthew 4:17

God asked Cain where his brother Abel was. Cain answered, "Am I my brother's guardian?" (Genesis 4:9) To how many of us today could God address the same question, and how many of us might give the same answer? Cain slew his brother because he envied him. We kill our brothers, slowly, deliberately, almost with malice aforethought. This is not because we, the affluent nations, envy other people. No, we left them in a state where no one can really envy them. We are killing, meting out death, not because of envy, but because of avarice and greed.

So much power and pain goes forth from this continent throughout the world. Technology becomes evil when it panders to the wealthy and doesn't care for the poor, when it helps those who have and makes envious those who have not.

We have given mere pennies for the raw materials of poor nations and charged dollars for the processed goods. We knew that without "purchase dollars" their standard of living would not improve, and that slowly, through much misery and pain, they would come to death by starvation or disease secondary to poverty. Then, we would put on the mask of charity, benignly bestowing a few million, or even billions that we could easily afford but which would not alleviate their misery.

Am I my brother's keeper? If we truly examined our Western conscience—the conscience of the so-called affluent society—we would be trembling indeed. It would be clear that we have slain our brother by enlarging our profits. Our profits! That is all we care about these days. Thousands of death-dealing planes and weapons of all kinds are being sold by most of the "affluent societies" to countries of the Middle East and elsewhere. We are delighted, because they prolong our own lives while the lives of others are destroyed in endless skirmishes and wars all over the world.

There is a fantastic violation of justice where capitalism through greed exploits the developing nations of the world. Materialism, worship of self, licentiousness, decadence are rampant. Decadence is what Assyria, Babylon, and ancient Rome died of, as history clearly indicates. Once a nation repudiates moral and ethical conduct, down the drain they go.

The agony of Christ continues.

All around the world millions of human beings are starving and dying. Why is it that massive relief from all countries, from everywhere, doesn't pour in from the hands of all those who have an abundance and who talk so constantly about love, about God?

Where love is, God is. But can God be present where there is no love? Is he absent, then, from nations that kill one another, waging hopeless wars that lead nowhere except to the death of thousands? "The agony of Christ continues unto the end of the world," wrote Pascal, the French philosopher. It continues in his Mystical Body. Whenever there is no love, Christ is rejected and killed again on a thousand Golgothas that are going on almost all over the globe with most of its people not even noticing.

In every large city of the Western world, the poor are still stretching out their hands for crumbs which fall from the rich man's table. Only a few crumbs fall to them. There is little love from the rich to the poor. Doesn't anyone see that in each of the poor it is Christ who begs?

When shall we who call ourselves Christians begin to be Christlike, and to love as he commanded us? "It is by your love for one another, that everyone will recognize you as my disciples." (John 13:35)

It has to begin with us.

Am I my brother's keeper? Am I being my brother's keeper? No. But at long last, my brothers of the poor nations are slowly gathering, gathering to face us. The confrontation will be terrible. For as we look at this incredibly immense gathering of our poor brothers, whom we have exploited to the limit of anybody's endurance, they will suddenly turn into the figure of Christ—all of them—Christ armed with cords. He will chase us, the traffickers in his temple, the moneylenders, the death-sellers, with the cords of his wrath we so justly deserve. (John 2:13–17)

Perhaps through a tremendous retrenchment, through poverty, through a whole series of events, people will turn to God and he will revive us. If twelve people could convert the world, what can we do? It's incredible. The options (to use a secular term) or the dream (in spiritual terms) are so immense and they are opening before us with such a clarity. But it has to begin with us. If we allow greed to enter our souls to the point of disregarding our neighbour, we, as a nation, will die. It's not the president or the senate that's going to bring about the change, it's you.

At a food conference in Italy there was reference to the Old Testament story of Joseph who was sold by his brothers to Pharaoh, and who eventually filled the granaries of Egypt to the full, so that when famine came there was enough to feed everybody. (Genesis 41:46–56) They said we need to make up a "granary" that everybody can go to, that suffices for the whole world. They soon realized that couldn't be done under capitalism, which has a profit motive.

But what we have to do is to gather into the barns of our heart those things that feed people, even beyond bread—God, his peace, his forgiveness, his understanding, his joy. We have to fill our hearts with these so that people can come and get faith, hope, and love—so as to survive. We need to put our hand to the plow.

Am I my brother's keeper? This is the question we have to ask. On our answer hinges our political, economic, and individual survival.

Christ calls us to repentance, so that he might bring us peace.

Whatever happened to the notion of sin? We have almost forgotten how to spell it, so little is it written or spoken about. Has it become an obsolete word, archaic? Or worse, has it become an indecent word, not to be mentioned among Christians, especially "enlightened" ones?

Is sin always an individual occurrence? Is it possible for there to be a collective, corporate sin? Looking down the long corridor of history one can find many instances of corporate sin in which a group of people, sometimes whole countries, participated.

The individual, under such circumstances, might appear to be sinless. Yet through participating in a corporate sin he may be guilty because he has lost the ability to judge between good and evil.

All who participated collectively in Hitler's Third Reich madness were guilty. As individuals, they didn't seem to harm anyone. But somehow or other they agreed to, or were involved in the heinous sin of exterminating six million Jews. Somehow they also participated in a mad orgy of trying to conquer the world. This was a collective sin, a corporate sin, for which a whole nation must atone, and is atoning.

So many people lately bring forth, for their exoneration, the fact that some superior, some commander-in-chief has ordered them to do this or that. They claim they were not responsible for what they did. Theirs was not a sin; on the contrary, it was an act of obedience, far removed from sin. As a soldier, to be involved in a mass killing of women and children because of an order from headquarters is to be involved in a corporate sin. The order should have been disregarded, even at the price of one's own life if need be.

It is time we recognize this collective kind of sin, especially in politics and government. We cannot ignore it. If we do, we submit to its consequences. We shall be sinning with the others.

The tragedy of scandals, political and others, is what happens to the integrity of the individuals involved. Like so many of Hitler's men, those involved simply "obeyed." They obeyed in spite of the fact that they sensed that obedience in this case was a grave sin, a collective sin against God and against others.

Corporate sin mars a nation's reputation for charity and compassion, undermines its Constitution and is an outrage to its democracy. Indeed, this calls for prayer.

My heart is breaking over the state of the world. I pray about the United States more than all the other countries. What is so tragic is that we have, in a manner of speaking, sold our soul to the devil. Not always, but still, we were self-centered. We wanted to do what we wanted to do, when we wanted, and that was tragic. We were interested in ourselves. We forgot our neighbour. Above all, we didn't listen to God. We didn't remember that he said, "Love one another as I have loved you." (John 13:34) We concentrated on ourselves. We looked for a buck, or for a fix, no matter what the cost.

I have been accused of not loving America because once in a while I am frank about her coming dangers, her materialism. But, a deep pity wells up in my heart for the Church in America. How thoroughly we got lost in the woods of compromise, worldly prudence, complacency, comfort, luxury. So clear before me is the chaos that reigns in our midst that all I can do, figuratively speaking, is weep over it.

Lord, why did you invite me to a ringside seat of your eternally renewed Passion, and that of the poor? Because of your love, you bring me to where I, an activist, can answer your call of love. So tiny be my answer, you still want it.

Catherine Doherty
Diary, 5 March 1942

Whenever we discuss the gospel we have an ability to rationalize. Intellectual seduction is one of the greatest sins. It is terrible to break faith, to rationalize away from Christ and his commandments to love—and then to influence another person to do the same. Yet those are the sins that are walking amongst us today, literally walking and calling, like some kind of a siren, calling us to betrayal of our very profound beliefs.

We need, today, a national repentance. We need the kind of repentance of times past when a lot of people got together and asked God's forgiveness for their sins, the sins of a city—perhaps because the city was besieged. Or as the Jews in the Old Testament tore their garments and covered themselves with ashes.

If there is anything today that we have to think about individually and collectively it's repentance. We need to repent before God, get his forgiveness, and then forgive ourselves and others. For we have sinned in arrogance and in pride, which have begotten violence and total disregard for any human act of pity, of tenderness, of understanding. Each of us carries the sin of the other. It is time we looked at it in depth, because a little later there may be no time left—someone, some place, will blow this earth open, in some way.

But Christ has risen from the dead. Christ is in our midst. He comes to us with tenderness, forgiveness, love, calling us to repentance, so that he might embrace us, so that he might bring us peace.

Depart from the selfishness of anxiety and guilt.

Am I my brother's keeper? I am my brother's killer.

No wonder we are caught in the net of our own guilt. It is a strange guilt. It is born of our inordinate desire for the good things of life, for a style of life that is almost barbarous in its hedonism. This begets a kind of guilt which does not allow the individual to be at peace with God, his fellowman, or even with himself.

We are used to our anxiety. We are secure in our selfishness, we do not want to mature, to accept the awesome, terrible, yet totally liberating freedom which comes when we enter the Law of Love which God gives us. Christ asks us to depart, with his grace, from our selfish existence of anxiety and guilt.

This is the time for stillness. Stand still and listen so that you can get perspective on your life according to God's plan. Everywhere people are grabbing, grabbing. Nobody feels they should do anything for anybody. Grabbing is avarice: "This is our gold, our oil, our water, our electricity." Instead of using the word "we" you hear everywhere the word "I." When nations and individuals reach that stage, they will fall apart, because the greatest sin before God is pride, and avarice is its handmaid. To grab for myself that which belongs to all is a grave and tragic sin.

Individuals as well as governments and nations are confronted with seemingly unsolvable situations. For example, in the midst of fantastic wealth the affluent nations are faced with a continuous, tragic, almost obscene poverty. Many Christians have realized that they have a personal responsibility for this poverty. They have confronted themselves and God as being "their brother's keeper." We are called to alleviate this poverty.

St. Thomas Aquinas has a saying to the effect that "a modicum of necessities is necessary to practice virtue," or, to put it in another way, "one cannot preach Christ to people with empty stomachs." On our home front, we need to meet these great problems with flexibility.

There are moments in our prayer life when God wants us to really use our intellect and present to him our problems, political, social, economic, technological, ecological, theological, philosophical. I approach God in prayer about everything and find that a new light is shed upon each thing, a new slant given, even if they are not all necessarily totally resolved.

One can get really interesting, valuable, and pertinent help through praying, which means presenting these problems to God. The light of the Holy Spirit is ours. He is the advocate of the Poor, and who of us is not in some way poor. Why shouldn't he illuminate and lead us toward some solution to these problems that confront humanity today?

Chapter 9

Evangelization

*Father, I am not asking you to remove them from the world,
but to protect them from the Evil One.
Consecrate them in the truth; your word is truth.
As you sent me into the world, I have sent them into the world,
and for their sake I consecrate myself
so that they too may be consecrated in truth.*

John 17:15, 17-19

Every Christian by baptism is an apostle. The world is his mission. He or she is supposed to bring the glad news and restore the kingdom of God within his or her neighbourhood, job, travels—in each social, personal, family, recreational contact.

It is against the backdrop of the tragic non-incarnation of Christ's teachings in the life of an average Christian that the Church is working today. Many persons cannot stand the hypocrisy that has developed around Christianity—the non-incarnation, the compromises, the rationalization of Christians against their own faith, the tremendous watering down of it. The non-Christian "isms" feed on that hypocrisy, personal, national, and international. It is still the weakness of the West which professes to be Christian and is not.

The tragic poverty of this world is indifference, rejection, and hatred toward Christ.

Not only all countries but our own backyards and the streets on which we live are mission territory, even as are our own hearts and minds and souls, and those of every neighbour. Success can be measured only in terms of love for one another.

Relieving physical poverty, though one of the most beautiful of the corporal works of mercy and the responsibility of all Christians, is not enough. In my later years, I've discovered more about the heart of poverty. I used to think of it as physical poverty, the poverty of those who are hungry, who are in need of food, clothing, and shelter. I'm still immensely concerned about them. We must always cherish those who suffer from physical needs, and take care of them. But the real poverty in this world is the poverty of those who have no faith, of those who do not believe in God. The poverty which my heart seeks to alleviate, the poor that my whole heart wants to enrich and to touch, are those who have no faith.

The deepest poverty lies in the rejection of Christ. The tragic poverty of this world is indifference to, and rejection and hatred of Christ. This kind of poverty, which mankind at the moment is subjecting itself to, is a bitter fruit. We need to go deeply into this. Atrocities are committed in God's name by those who do not know better and who call him by the name of Allah or Yahweh or Christ. These are not in truth, because they do not recognize his face. We are moving into a darkness created by men who have ceased to believe in God.

Real poverty is not knowing who God is. God died for us, loves us, and walks in our midst as one of us. Christ has not left this earth, though he has gone to his Father.

Christ bids us to let him make of us a healing tool for his Mystical Body, the Church, wherever we are. We will heal, console, and bring multitudes to God.

We are called to leave behind our narrowness, a type of superiority, a sort of nationalism.

My brothers and sisters in Christ, I implore you before it is too late, clothe the skeletons of your flesh with the love of Christ. If we do, we can lead the world and humanity out of the terrible and hellish depths to which it has sunk. There is so little time.

Being our brother's keeper cannot be limited to one's own country or one's own people. To the Christian, all men are brothers and hence to be looked after, loved and helped. Today the whole world is mission territory.

Developing countries often receive reluctantly, if at all, those who come from richer countries, for they are considered paternalistic, and also, they can always return from whence they came, at a moment's notice, while the reverse is often not possible for those of the host country. It is essential that we all step softly, especially in multi-cultural situations. We need to beg the Holy Spirit to guide us through the forest of different cultures.

We live in an age of tremendous upheaval and change, an age of war, nationalism and hatreds. When we come to serve our brothers and sisters in Christ in another part of the world, it is essential that we walk in grave humility, with a heart full of gratitude that we have been permitted entrance into our host country.

At the same time, although our world is certainly experiencing the storms of national and international turmoil, we also need to pay very great attention to our own countries, for these are mission territories, as well. The distinction between foreign missions and home missions has been blurred, because the de-Christianization of people in the Western world is too evident to deny. It is urgent that we pledge ourselves to restore at least a small portion of it to God. How tragic and pitiful it is that people cannot experience the inner peace which is their heritage from Christ. This seems especially true of Western people, most of whom are baptized and grafted onto the Body of Christ.

In our own country, as well, we are called to leave behind our narrowness, a type of unconscious superiority, a sort of nationalism. We need to gird ourselves with the ability to adjust and to open our hearts ever wider. Our cities are becoming more cosmopolitan and the differences in mores, language, attitudes spring unbidden before our eyes, but it is imperative that we believe that we are all brothers and sisters under the skin, all parts of one humanity. We need to be watchful to stress the positive in other cultures and heedful to avoid negative comments.

> *Evangelization is...the deepest identity of the Church; she exists in order to evangelize.*
>
> Pope Paul VI
> December 8, 1975

We tend to desire to shape people into the image of our own culture, our own group. We relate with others only according to our own experience, and it takes a long painful ascent up the rugged mountain of the Lord to see the full vision of the Christian apostolate as exemplified by Christ and his Father through the Holy Spirit. From this summit, we see that God loved the whole world, all of humanity, so much that he died for it. We see that we are called to be crucified with Christ.

Christians have the answer. Why don't we make it available?

Across the Western world, men and women are seeking mystical experiences of all kinds. Lately there is much influence in North America of ancient non-Christian Oriental religions and their New Age adaptations, for example, theosophy.

Each of us comes from a country or place which shaped us. The majority of North American people come from a deeply religious background which has shaped them through two millennia and it is well nigh impossible to completely discard it. All of us of European stock are molded by our religion. We might discard it and think we got rid of it, but we didn't.

Especially since the '60s there has been a desire to sweep away the religions of parents and forefathers, and so a vacuum was created. Today we again have a pre-evangelical state facing us. It is a tragic situation. But it doesn't do to try to mix ancient religions or New Age with our Christian religion.

Across the whole world one can almost feel the growth of the Prince of Darkness. Actually, Satan doesn't grow; what allows him to "grow," to expand his influence, are people. Each person who accepts him, increases him. Witches and witchcraft abound. People are succumbing to evil, entering into evil ways of worship via strange rituals, opening themselves to the spirit that is inimical to Christ. Evil is permeating science and technology in the shape of greed, among other things, greed that is nearly ruining our earth. While people are into witchcraft, in service of the demon, we Christians have the answer. Why don't we make it available so people don't miss the big swath that is right in front of them?

We who are Catholics or Eastern Christians have the Eucharist and the beautiful prayers of our traditions. This is our habitat, the place we have to begin to make our own. The spirituality of both Roman Catholicism and the Christian East, the Fathers of the Church, the prophets of the Old Testament and the Psalms, the gospel, the lives of the saints, these we ought to be studying and leaving the other alone.

Our heads are easily turned by every fad that comes along, but let us stick with the treasure that is ours. This doesn't mean we don't study other religions but we need to be aware that when we delve into some of them we open ourselves to many dark forces which we perhaps don't know how to handle.

Be ready to follow Christ wherever he goes.

As we approach the call to evangelize and spread the Good News we need to be extremely flexible in what we do and be attentive to new opportunities, openings, possibilities, that cut across our preconceived notions and beckon into ways and situations that we have barely assessed or perhaps never thought of. Be prepared for constant changes. We cannot be rigid in any way or undesirous of change. We seek a deeper impenetration or presentation of the Good News. It is important for us to use all modern means of communication and technology to put across the message of Christ.

Flexibility needs to be prepared for by observing, thinking, researching, and prayer. But it is important that we do all these together, as a united community. We need to beg the Holy Spirit to lead us in the right direction. If we look for the paths that God is already laying out for us, a new awareness, a new vitality, and new sense of challenge and adventure will come into our hearts. We need to be ready to follow Christ wherever he goes, for Christ has a way of going into unexpected places. He often directs us toward an end that we don't yet perceive but that is just around the corner.

Discover people's real needs through friendship.

One of my techniques in loving others is what I call the "chit-chat apostolate," a homey person-to-person approach. It is a way of loving, of discovering the real needs of people, whether material or spiritual or any other, and our group always engaged in it. The chit-chat apostolate is but another way of speaking of friendships that are formed apparently casually, yet not so casually. When one is walking or traveling, one can be filled with one's own thoughts and unconcerned about the people one meets. Or, one can love and be concerned about everyone, every step of the way.

Out of this chit-chat apostolate the intangibles come forth, and one identifies with the people, which is the hardest part of any apostolate. At first, chit-chat seems to be a fragile suspension bridge to the other, but slowly it becomes a solid, well-built steel span of friendship. Always I've tried to promote the person to person approach.

People are often afraid to meet the other person, the stranger. The inner freedom to open a conversation is achieved by prayer. This personal approach is effective. We need to reach out to people, person to person. The chit-chat apostolate is essential to friendship, to brotherhood.

Along with chit-chat comes our identification with the poor, both in our hearts and in the way we live. We are poor with the poor, as Christ was. An incredible inner strength comes through being weak with the weak.

We are called to live out our friendship, in the market place if need be. We go about it very quietly, without any hurry. For if we wish to bind ourselves by this precious friendship, we need to take root where the other roots himself. We must become all to all in our love and daily service to them.

Evangelization

Being on fire with the love of God will set sparks in the heart of another.

Our world is poised at the stage of utter destruction and disaster. But we can uphold the world, that is, God upholds it in us, when we give God a place, a spot on which to put his strong hands and move through us. The place may be a tiny spot in this world. We need to open ourselves to him.

It is our own being on fire with the love of God that will set sparks in the hearts of others. We are called to accept the crucifixion of patience, which is the first defining characteristic of love in St. Paul's hymn. Even a few drops of love, of charity, are significant in a sea of complacency, indifference, or poverty. We lay people are also "priestly people." We are mediators between humanity and God. We are called to be a bridge on which others may travel to him.

God wants to use us as he used the uncouth, unlearned disciples for whom he thanked God saying, "I bless you, Father, Lord of heaven and earth, for hiding these things from the learned and the clever and revealing them to mere children." (Matthew 11:25) May we desire to be those little ones and to be used by him, no matter the cost to us.

We come to love, to be present among people. Our love expresses itself in hospitality, availability, charity, and peace. When one loves, one sees the needs of others and sets about to fulfill them humbly, reverently, quietly, without fanfare. Our homes can be places of love, hospitality. They can become a listening post where people come to be refreshed in spirit.

You will falter, stumble, fall—but don't stay down.

You will falter, you will stumble, you will fall. But don't stay down. Don't compromise. Keep cooperating with the tremendous graces God gives you. All we can give of ourselves is our poverty and God's love chaliced in that personal poverty. The poorer we are, the faster he comes to fill us. He is attracted when we acknowledge our poverty.

We might not see results. I might listen to people and nothing happens. I don't cure anybody, I don't counsel anyone. To come to the point of never seeing results is an excruciating thing. But to allow God to take away results that were visible is super-excruciating. God has to smash me completely so that I never think of results. It's devastating until one learns to live at that level of faith.

Receptivity is something God creates, by emptying you. You may not be so heroic as to empty yourself, but you allow yourself to be emptied. God removes from you all that is not of him.

Witness to Christ by your presence, by the way you sit, talk, eat.

A missionary's entry into his host country ought normally to be very unobtrusive. He or she will attract many people simply by prayer and apostolic chit-chat. There is much to recommend in Father Jacques Loew's book, *As If He Had Seen the Invisible: A Portrait of the Apostle Today*. We need to begin to contact people one by one, telling about ourselves and humbly, gently, and delicately asking about the other. Then we will discover the presence of God in them.

Remember that as Christians we are called to be apostles of the Good News continually, everywhere. We witness to Christ by our presence, by the way we sit, talk, eat. We evangelize at every second of the day and with each breath we take.

Especially when we are in Muslim countries, we need to avoid using dress and gestures that offend, even though in our own culture—in North America, or wherever, they would not be considered inappropriate. In fact, they might be considered quite modest here. Remember that the woman of the East is protected by fathers, brothers, uncles, the family, and the clan. Chastity of glance, of walk, of dress, of gesture, and speech is very important.

In an inimical milieu, hateful words, like stones, may be hurled at you. People can crucify you by their glances, by rejection, nonacceptance, and ridicule. Do not expect people in disparate cultures to be cordial or sympathetic toward you. They may dislike you on sight, if you are Westerners. You are that other who for centuries kept them down and who is really the instigator of their present goals, for your race drained their country for its own profit.

Being unprepared as to the points of pain and attack can lead to deep hurt. Some of the hates have been smouldering for centuries and now are free to find their desired objects. We may find ourselves in a desert of erupting hostilities, which for centuries have been trampled down and hidden in the subconscious and unconscious psyches of people who have never been free to openly express those hostilities to their masters, white men, Westerners, or so-called Christians.

The quality of an apostle who is the child of Christ's love is empathy, which means putting yourself in the place of the other, feeling what they feel and thinking like they think. Love alone can do such things. We Christians must learn to do this with all our might, through prayer, mortification, and more prayer. People's souls have been burdened with terrible hurt from centuries of maltreatment at the hands of the very people that you may represent. We are called to enter into this passion. We are called to atone.

When I first started my apostolate of Friendship House, in Harlem, New York, I was not accepted. I was accused of many kinds of immorality and sin, of being a communist. Even the police were initially against me. I was nearly friendless except for God, and I was penniless. Very many times I was spit upon, straight in the face. I was pelted with stones, wounded in the head, had a bone broken, and received many physical bruises. I walked for years in the cold hate of a world that did not understand what I stood for or who I was, and there were few on my side except God, his blessed Mother and the saints. And even these seemed very distant at the time. The evil one was close by.

Yes, I have gone this way. And I desire to convey in ordinary human words that in times of trial, so terribly much depends upon our perseverance. The plan of God and the Church depend on it.

Christ is the most radical person. We are rooted in him.

Every Christian is called by baptism to be an apostle. But God evidently desires that some of these lay Christians do a little more. He wants them to be special commando forces in his army of baptized Christians. So, he calls them either to a temporary commitment or to a life of permanent commitment. He wants them better trained, gives them special graces, and in the case of a permanent commitment, the special vocation of living the consecrated lay life.

Thomas Merton once said that the lay apostolate was the spearhead of Vatican II. All those little lay groups that laboured in various countries, and who took upon themselves poverty, chastity, and obedience, without any vows—they tired themselves out, they were heroic. They were pushed around, they were silenced, they were abolished, but they renewed themselves again and again. Out of this came something. These groups were all called radical in their early years. The most radical person ever was always Christ. We are rooted in him.

More and more, in various countries, young people are founding little communities of consecrated lay life which, in their consecration, resemble that of religious orders. This growing trickle may seem small, unimportant, hardly worth writing about. But these young people are proof that hope is with us. To those who have eyes to see and ears to hear, there is an underground swell, but it is quiet and very gentle.

In the line of apostles, we may see ourselves as the smallest, but like David slaying Goliath with only a smooth stone, Christ comes with the sling of his grace, bends down into the brook of life and picks up little pebbles—you and me—to place in his sling and slay whatever evil he wishes. Much humility, death to self, and love go into making those pebbles smooth.

To give an example from my own life, when I came as a refugee to North America in the '20s, a new civilization was being born after World War I. The rat race we know so well now was beginning to be felt. In the large American cities, conformity was evident, as well as a constantly growing materialism and the breakdown of the family—and the breaking up of old traditions. There was little peace.

I wanted to get away from these negative influences and to restore and preserve what was good in the past. In my mind, it was tied up with religion: with the liturgy and with the peace of God purchased through the works of one's hands, not only of one's brains. My heart wanted so much to restore the world to Christ.

Through his commandment to love, God gave us the Beatitudes and the corporal and spiritual works of mercy.

Also, I was aghast at the soupiness, the indifference of many Canadian and American Catholics and their ignorance as to what was transpiring in their lands. I realized very early during my first years as a refugee that there were dead-end streets in Canada and America, because I lived on them. I knew that the name of Christ, and he crucified, was not heard on the thousands of dead-end streets. That reduced my soul to an agony I have no words to describe. It shocked my youth and made me aware of the tremendous tragedy of the American and Canadian Catholics who seem to be dead asleep. They are not giving God to their fellowman, nor love.

Through witnessing the conquest of those dead-end streets by communists and other elements inimical to Christianity, I grew in my desire to fight materialism, atheism, communism, neo-paganism, and all the other "isms" that hindered Catholicism and Christianity in general—to fight them with the only weapons I thought worthy of using and capable of conquering. These isms were spawns of the children of hate. The only weapon that can conquer hate is love. My vocation was to love. I wanted to be in the front lines of this formidable battle. In the spirit of love, I, as well as the other members of the Friendship Houses I founded, would go where there were needs and allow love and its ingenuity to answer those needs.

When we began working with transient men during the Great Depression, we entered the field of social service. To us, it meant highly personalized service to the poor, and neighbourly help shot through with *caritas* or love. We understood that if we were to prove our love of God we had to love our neighbour.

Patience, as well as time, are required in order to listen to the poor, who are inarticulate, who take a long time to express themselves and a longer time to state their real needs. Somehow the ingenuity of love always found the precious commodity—time—to listen and, thereby, to lessen the load that can kill faster than a disease.

As one listens, one evaluates how best to help. In one's relating to the poor, one should be subjective, according to the Beatitudes, mourn with those who mourn. (Matthew 5:5)

Once one begins to work with people it becomes inevitable that one gets involved with the whole person, the human being with all his needs, joys, and pains. The worker who seeks employment and the economic security to fill his needs, the Christian who knows that he needs God and wants to know him, the citizen who is part of the political system of a country.

To deal with each person means to deal with the mind, heart, and soul, as well as the body. Thus, I think that God gave us, through his commandment to love, the Beatitudes and both the corporal and spiritual works of mercy. These are so interwoven that they can never be separated. They embrace the whole person.

The empty side of the cross, the side Christ is not hanging on, is for you.

In the first flush of emotional religious enthusiasm, it is easy to say, "I will go and work with the poor for the love of God." But in the crucible of every day that initial fervour won't last. Stark and alone, the cross finally makes its appearance; and the lay apostle suddenly realizes that the empty side, the side on which Christ does not hang, is meant for himself or herself. We too are called to be "lifted up," with Christ, (John 12:32) so as to draw all things, all persons, to him.

I need to prepare myself to be ridiculed, hated, and even persecuted in an underhand way through gossip and rumours. I can expect a lack of cooperation at first, in any endeavour I might undertake. Love, patience, perseverance, understanding, and trust will be my weapons.

When we come to a place where even the ordinary necessities of life are lacking, it is obvious that we will direct our primary attention to fulfilling those needs. But we need to remember that human beings do not live on bread alone. (Matthew 4:4) We are all apostles to one another. Each of us is to proclaim the Good News to the other, repeatedly, because the application of the gospel is not easy.

Evangelization

Our apostolic life and works take sustenance from the bishop of the diocese.

It is not easy to know with your whole mind, body, and soul that you have to preach the gospel with your life, without any compromise, to identify yourself with the other in love, and to have empathy and understanding for those you serve. It is not easy to have your heart, mind, and soul cry out that you are compelled to go where nobody else wants to go, to the most forgotten, most despised, and downtrodden people.

It is one thing to do this by the impenetration of grace into your own heart, soul, and mind, and it is another to find words to transmit this into the minds and hearts and souls of others. You have to battle through muck and prejudice people don't know they have. It is not easy.

Yet, these were not the main difficulties I encountered in transmitting the spirit to the volunteers and members of our lay apostolate, or in organizing the training. The main difficulty was that there was no canonical standing in the Church for lay apostolic groups. There were no vows or promises, then. There could not be, because, canonically, there was no one to "receive" them. Yet strangely, from the beginning I felt I was committing myself for life. First, to the Apostolate, and secondly to a life of poverty, chastity, and obedience, without vows or with private vows made to my confessor.

But a deep spiritual understanding of the "Counsels of Perfection," as the vows were called, was hard to transmit to American and Canadian minds. They were trained, impregnated, filled with the image of men and women—religious—as the only totally dedicated persons. To come to the idea of lay people living fully the life of the Counsels, both in spirit and in fact, and without vows was utterly incomprehensible. Europe had a tradition of single people, and groups as well, living this way. But it was not so in North America.

Whatever apostolic life we lived and works we were engaged in, took their spiritual sustenance and effectiveness from one fact only— that they were given us by the bishop to whom we gave obedience.

There are many intangibles in the tinder-like atmosphere in which we work which are ready to burst into flames at any minute.

We battle walls of prejudice, ignorance, and people's inability to communicate with one another. We need to be ready to break the walls down, but gently. The walls can be taken apart, brick by brick, or log by log, and the materials thus obtained can be used to build a bridge of understanding.

Chapter 10

Ecumenical Bridges

*Anyone who does the will of my Father in heaven
is my brother and sister and mother.*

Matthew 12:50

Ecumenism has become fashionable, but I practised it way back when it was not in vogue. From the time I first came to Canada, I was a pioneer in the ecumenical movement and sponsored it wherever possible, with regard to the Eastern Churches, through bringing in speakers, as well as lecturing and writing about these extensively, myself. I helped to build and establish the Russian Orthodox Church in Toronto and was actively involved in ecumenism with Protestants. I also worked toward unity with the Jewish people. I present my own experience as an example.

Love, who is God, is the only answer.

Our very life can be ecumenical, a place of encounter with Christ in each person who passes through it. We are called to build bridges, to be a bridge between disparate peoples.

Love can bridge the gap between Catholics, Jews, Muslims, Protestants. We all believe in one God, the God of love. In every person, there is God, and God is in every person, because he died to save all people. Why then can we not live by the law of his love? What is stopping us?

Love can bridge the gap between Christians and Jews. After all, we Christians are spiritual Semites and the Old Testament was the forerunner of the New. The Love of the Father became incarnate for us, and he, Christ, was a son of Abraham.

Why can't we believe that only Love, who is God, can walk upon the stormy waters of our times and quiet them? Love is the only answer, and it has to start in the mind and heart of each person. Only then will it be effective. Then the whole world will enter into its springtime, the storms will be hushed, and peace will reign among us.

From *The Documents of Vatican II* regarding ecumenism:

Although the Catholic Church has been endowed with all divinely revealed truth and with all means of grace, yet its members fail to live by them with all the fervour that they should, so that the radiance of the Church's image is less clear in the eyes of our separated brethren and of the world at large, and the growth of God's kingdom is delayed. All Catholics must therefore aim at Christian perfection and, each according to his station, play his part that the Church may daily be more purified and renewed. For the Church must bear in her own body the humility and dying of Jesus, against the day when Christ will present her to Himself in all her glory without spot or wrinkle....

Catholics must gladly acknowledge and esteem the truly Christian endowments from our common heritage which are to be found among our separated brethren. It is right and salutary to recognize the riches of Christ and virtuous works in the lives of others who are bearing witness to Christ, sometimes even to the shedding of their blood. For God is always wonderful in His works and worthy of all praise.

Nor should we forget that anything wrought by the grace of the Holy Spirit in the hearts of our separated brethren can be a help to our own edification. Whatever is truly Christian is never contrary to what genuinely belongs to the faith; indeed, it can always bring a deeper realization of the mystery of Christ and the Church....

This Sacred Council is gratified to note that the participation by the Catholic faithful in ecumenical work is growing daily. It commends this work to the bishops everywhere in the world to be vigorously stimulated by them and guided with prudence....

There can be no ecumenism worthy of the name without a change of heart. For it is from renewal of the inner life of our minds, from self-denial and an unstinted love that desires of unity take their rise and develop in a mature way. We should therefore pray to the Holy Spirit for

Ecumenical Bridges

the grace to be genuinely self-denying, humble, gentle in the service of others, and to have an attitude of brotherly generosity towards them.... So we humbly beg pardon of God and of our separated brethren, just as we forgive them that trespass against us....

All the faithful should remember that the more effort they make to live holier lives according to the Gospel, the better will they further Christian unity and put it into practice. For the closer their union with the Father, the Word, and the Spirit, the more deeply and easily will they be able to grow in mutual brotherly love.

This change of heart and holiness of life, along with public and private prayer for the unity of Christians, should be regarded as the soul of the whole ecumenical movement, and merits the name, 'spiritual ecumenism'....

It is a recognized custom for Catholics to have frequent recourse to that prayer for the unity of the Church which the Saviour Himself on the eve of His death so fervently appealed to His Father: 'That they may all be one.'

The apostolate of unity is one of suffering and love.

Ever since I left Russia in my late teens, I felt in my heart a deep sorrow, the sorrow of division in the Church between East and West. For to me the Church was always one. The words of Christ reverberated in my mind and heart constantly, "May they all be one, just as, Father...we are one." (John 17:21–22)

In my childhood, my family lived out the traditions of both the Russian Orthodox Church and the Catholic Church. I prayed again and again, prostrated before Christ, that some solution be found by which we shall become one as he desired. I spent years explaining and teaching, here in the West, about the Eastern Church and traditions.

The split between East and West was always predominately cultural and political. However, I do not wish to dwell on reasons for the split. What my heart desires is unity. The circumstances of my childhood made of me a sort of bridge between the two, even before I knew the depths and heights of the split—which came to me in full force when I came to the North American continent where, to my amazement, the Eastern Rites of the Catholic Church were widely considered to be heretical, and where ignorance about them was profound, abysmal, almost total.

I knew that I had a share in the healing of this division in the body of Christ, and I have lived my Eastern spirituality and shared whatever knowledge I could with my fellow Roman Catholics over the years, through writing and experience. In the early days, I met with tremendous hostilities over this. I contributed often to magazines, telling of the European movement of unity between East and West, specifically with the Russian Orthodox Church.

Years came and went. Nothing happened. Then came Vatican II, and suddenly people in North America were talking about icons and placing them in their homes. Russian theological books became popular.

The apostolate of unity is one of suffering and love. It blends, melts, becomes one with the crucifixion of Russia, with the pain of the Eastern Romanian Church, with the division of the Greek Church, with the pain experienced by the Malabars in India through centuries of Roman persecution, with the derision and condescension felt by the faithful of the Coptic Church and in a special way with the wound inflicted historically by the Roman Rite on the Eastern minority in Canada and the U.S.A.

The essence of Eastern spirituality is the Liturgy, the gospel, and therefore *caritas,* including love for one's enemies. For the persecuted ones who forgive their enemies and love them are like unto Christ and bring to this continent his mercy, his forgiveness, and his love. People's hearts need to be opened, not first to a spirituality, nor to East or West, but to Christ.

From *The Documents of Vatican II* regarding the Eastern Churches:

> Among other matters of great importance, it is a pleasure for this Council to remind everyone that there flourish in the East many particular or local Churches, among which the Patriarchal Churches hold first place, and of these not a few pride themselves in tracing their origins back to the apostles themselves....
>
> Similarly it must not be forgotten that from the beginning the Churches of the East have had a treasury from which the Western Church has drawn extensively—in liturgical practice, spiritual tradition, and law. Nor must we undervalue the fact that it was the ecumenical councils held in the East that defined the basic dogmas of the Christian faith, on the Trinity, on the Word of God Who took flesh of the Virgin

Mary. To preserve this faith these Churches have suffered and still suffer much....

Everyone also knows with what great love the Christians of the East celebrate the sacred liturgy, especially the Eucharistic celebration, source of the Church's life and pledge of future glory, in which the faithful, united with their bishop, have access to God the Father through the Son, the Word made flesh, Who suffered and has been glorified, and so, in the outpouring of the Holy Spirit, they enter into communion with the most holy Trinity, being made 'sharers of the divine nature.' Hence, through the celebration of the Holy Eucharist in each of these churches, the Church of God is built up and grows in stature and through concelebration, their communion with one another is made manifest.

In this liturgical worship, the Christians of the East pay high tribute, in beautiful hymns of praise, to Mary ever Virgin, whom the ecumenical Council of Ephesus solemnly proclaimed to be the holy Mother of God, so that Christ might be acknowledged as being truly Son of God and Son of Man, according to the Scriptures. Many also are the saints whose praise they sing, among them the Fathers of the universal Church.

These Churches, although separated from us, yet possess true sacraments and above all, by apostolic succession, the priesthood and the Eucharist, whereby they are linked with us in closest intimacy....

Moreover, in the East are found the riches of those spiritual traditions which are given expression especially in monastic life. There from the glorious times of the holy Fathers, monastic spirituality flourished, which then later flowed over into the Western world, and there provided the source from which Latin monastic life took its rise and has drawn fresh vigour ever since. Catholics therefore are earnestly recommended to avail themselves of the spiritual riches of the Eastern Fathers which lift up the whole man to the contemplation of the divine.

The very rich liturgical and spiritual heritage of the Eastern Churches should be known, venerated, preserved, and cherished by all. They must recognize that this is of supreme importance for the faithful preservation of the fullness of Christian tradition, and for bringing about reconciliation between Eastern and Western Christians.

Already from the earliest times the Eastern Churches followed their own forms of ecclesiastical law and custom, which were sanctioned by the approval of the Fathers of the Church, of synods, and even of ecumenical councils. Far from being an obstacle to the Church's unity, a certain diversity of customs and observances only adds to her splendour, and is of great help in carrying out her mission, as has already been stated. To remove, then, all shadow of doubt, this holy Council solemnly declares that the Churches of the East, while remembering the necessary unity of the whole Church, have the power to govern themselves according to the disciplines proper to them, since these are better suited to the character of their faithful, and more for the good of their souls. The perfect observance of this traditional principle not always indeed carried out in practice, is one of the essential prerequisites for any restoration of unity....

Where the authentic theological traditions of the Eastern Church are concerned, we must recognize the admirable way in which they have their roots in Holy Scripture, and how they are nurtured and given expression in the life of the liturgy. They derive their strength too from the living tradition of the apostles and from the works of the Fathers and spiritual writers of the Eastern Churches. Thus they promote the right ordering of Christian life and, indeed, pave the way to a full vision of Christian truth.

All this heritage of spirituality and liturgy, of discipline and theology, in its various traditions, this holy synod declares to belong to the full Catholic and apostolic character of the Church....

It is the Council's urgent desire that, in the various organizations and living activities of the Church, every effort should be made toward the gradual realization of this unity, especially by prayer, and by fraternal dialogue on points of doctrine and the more pressing pastoral problems of our time. Similarly, the Council commends to the shepherds and faithful of the Catholic Church to develop closer relations with those who are no longer living in the East but are far from home, so that friendly collaboration with them may increase, in the spirit of love, to the exclusion of all feeling of rivalry or strife. If this cause is wholeheartedly promoted, the Council hopes that the barrier dividing the Eastern Church and Western Church will be removed, and that at last there may be but the one dwelling, firmly established on Christ Jesus, the cornerstone, who will make both one.

A Prayer to the Mother of God, the Mother of All People

The following prayer is addressed to Our Lady of Combermere, the title under which the Mother of God is particularly honoured in Madonna House.

Beloved Mary, Our Lady of Combermere, you are the Mother of all men and women, for your Son has made you so. When he was dying on the cross, he gave you to St. John, and he gave St. John to you. In one gesture he who was not able to make any gestures, because he was crucified, made you the Mother of everyone. We are all your children. Unseen, you bend down tenderly over each one of us.

If we would only pause for a moment, if we would only quiet our poor minds and enter your great silence, we would know how lovingly you hold us in your arms. In these days so many of your children are fragmented; so many wish to die; so many do not know where they are going; so many are refugees, lost in the immense deserts of our huge cities.

Take pity on us, for we are the most pitiful people ever. You see us—Catholics, Orthodox, Protestants, Jews, Muslims, Buddhists, Hindus, peoples of all religions. You see every one of us and, whereas the arms of your Son were crucified, yours are outstretched to embrace the whole world. Your arms are ready to hold any of us who come to you. You are always a Mother, for you have been created to be the Mother of God and of all people. So we come to you, first bowing low before the Father, the Son, and the Holy Spirit, making upon ourselves the sign of the Holy Cross. In this, we find our healing.

Chapter 11

Unity in the Trinity

> I have given them the glory you gave me, that they may be one as we are one. With me in them and you in me, may they be so perfected in unity that the world will recognize that it was you who sent me and that you have loved them as you have loved me.
>
> ~~Luke 6:20~~
> JOHN 22:23

Where should renewal lead first and foremost? It ought to lead Christians to become a community of love. God said, "It is not right that the man should be alone." (Genesis 2:18) God knew about communities of love. The first and eternal community of love is the Most Holy Trinity. Each individual Christian has first to become part of their community of love, part of the Trinity. We are called to incarnate this union in daily life. Then, each of us can form a community of love with everyone we meet. Other people may be strangers to us, but a stranger is simply a friend I haven't yet met. Friendship is the fruit of love.

Each family is called to become a community with its neighbours, that is, with that part of the world which enters into the orbit of their family's ordinary relationships. Always, we are to begin with ourselves. We are called to undergo a *metanoia*, a change of heart, an emptying of our self, so that the divine light which comes through unity with the Holy Trinity may flow through us and draw others into that light.

The eternal community is the Holy Trinity. It has existed eternally, having no beginning and no end. The community of the Trinity is simply the community of love: God the Father loving God the Son and this love bringing forth the Holy Spirit.

In order to form a community, we first need to make contact with the Holy Trinity. Then and only then, can we make a community with our fellowmen. How do we make contact? No one can blueprint this for us, but there are basically two elements involved: prayer and ourselves. We can find God through one another because Christ's incarnation brought all humanity into himself and he entered into all of humanity. Because of the incarnation, we have been readmitted to the community of the Trinity, to the community of love.

Sobornost begins in the hearts of people whose prayer lives are spent before the Trinity and reflect the Father, Son, and Holy Spirit.

A new word has made its appearance in Catholic magazines. It is a word very familiar to those of Eastern Christian traditions—*"sobornost."*

"Sobor" generally means a cathedral, usually the one where the bishop of the diocese is in residence, and where, on all major occasions, his priests and people gather around him to offer the Eucharist and to praise God.

"Sobrania" means a gathering, in a sense somewhat similar to the word liturgy, which is basically a gathering of people to perform some kind of communal work.

Sobornost, though having *sobrania* (gathering) as a root, has a much different connotation. It has some kinship with the English word "collegiality," yet it is as far removed from this word as the earth is from the moon. It has a much more profound meaning for Eastern Christians.

Sobornost is not a word to be used flippantly. This is a special hazard today when so many foreign words are entering our language. It is a very holy word, an awesome word. *Sobornost* has great depths, and its incarnation into the lives of people is something like a spring that wells up from the very heart of the most Holy Trinity.

Perhaps the reality of the Holy Trinity provides the best context in which to approach the true meaning of *sobornost*. For in the Trinitarian life, there is complete and total unanimity of heart and mind, if one can express it that way. *Sobornost* begins in the hearts of people whose prayer lives are spent before the Trinity and who are a reflection of the Father, Son, and Holy Spirit.

Those who act within the ideal of *sobornost* become lovers and servants of one another.

When the people of God truly become bound, as all Christians are called to be, by the will of the Father into a community, they take on the obedience of the Son, and they rely for total unity of mind and heart on the Holy Spirit, the Advocate, whom the Father sent to remind us of all that the Son has taught.

Sobornost, therefore, is a unity of mind, heart, and soul among Christians who truly desire to preach the gospel with their lives, to clothe it with their own flesh. *Sobornost* is the manifestation of that unity Christ asked us to live and reflect when he prayed, "May they may all be one, just as, Father, you are in me and I am in you." (John 17:21)

Sobornost creates among the faithful neither dependence on authority nor independence, nor even interdependence. It calls for life on much higher spiritual planes and levels. It calls for a oneness in the Body of Christ. We are called to be so totally one with him, and hence with the Father and the Holy Spirit, as to become in truth a Trinitarian body, ourselves.

Sobornost is achieved by intense and constant prayer. The function of authority in such a community—whether bishops, priests, or fathers and mothers—is that of suffering servants of Yahweh. (Isaiah 42, 49, 50, 52) Just as Christ was, they too are to become people of the towel, basin, and water, for Christians can wash the feet of each person, even as Christ washed the feet of his apostles. (John 13:1–17)

Within the spiritual understanding of *sobornost,* authority is the servant of all, willingly crucified for the needs and the salvation of all. Authority is in love with God and others. Members of a community functioning within the ideal of *sobornost* would be lovers and servants of one another. Together, they would be constantly alert to and aware of one thing—that they are not many, but one in the Lord. Love alone can achieve that mysterious unity that comes only from the person of Jesus Christ, encountered and become one with us.

It is Christ who brings about oneness.

We are an integral part of one another. What binds us together is love and love alone. Love is a Person, love is God.

Whatever form a Christian's prayer takes, the whole body of Christ, the people of God, are present within him. He just cannot pray "alone."

Sobornost is a mystery given us by God as the gospel solution to the deep spiritual problems that confront families, religious communities, communities of consecrated laity—and perhaps someday the community of Christian nations.

Its mystery can only be approached and achieved through prayer. *Sobornost* finds its roots, its essence, its very reason for being in the Holy Sacrifice of the Mass. It is Christ who brings about oneness, and all of us together are united in his love for us, our love for him and our love for one another.

At one time, though, I began to worry about the constant experimentation in liturgical renewal. *Avant-garde* Masses are interesting, but they soon pale. Change is exciting, but man cannot live on change alone. Change must be a road leading to the essence. Experimentation didn't seem to be bringing forth the expected results. It didn't seem to be forming a community of love among those who were offering the sacrifice and those who participated in it—those who had received the Lord together.

I listened to the comments of learned theologians, of eminent liturgists, and of rank and file religious. I listened to avant-garde groups, the ones who are in on all the latest things. I listened to those who were not "in."

Coming as I do from Russia, with the Eastern accent of the Church being part of my very being, my thinking and my faith, I felt there was something in the ongoing renewal of the Church that didn't quite seem right, especially in the liturgical renewal.

Most people seemed to think that what was important were the nonessentials. Many persons confused nonessentials with essentials, and seemed themselves to be confused. People attending the most *avant-garde* Masses would leave the Church without talking to one another, without welcoming the stranger in their midst. It was as if they had enjoyed themselves immensely and felt a oneness with others during the liturgy but afterward, in some strange way, they reverted back to being private individuals.

It took me a long time to realize what I was up against. I had been brought up with a very simple idea which was and is part of my faith: because he is a Christian, a Christian is never alone.

Do I recite the rosary alone or with others? Am I engaged in some vocal prayers? Am I making the Way of the Cross by myself? Do I enter total solitude? Do I read the word of God and contemplate the Lord in a chapel or in my room? It doesn't matter, really. At all times and always the whole Christian community, the whole world of humanity, is with me, present to me. I pray that we never confuse the nonessential with what is essential.

Don't stop trying.

The ideal that needs to be realized is *sobornost,* the community that forms one complete, indivisible whole to which you always belong, from which you can never be separated, precisely because you are mysteriously one with all the others who form that *sobornost.*

The Western world, people of the North American continent in particular, seem to value very much individualism, their sense of individuality. In recent years, however, the concept of the Mystical Body of Christ has begun to penetrate people's thinking. Now the phrase "people of God" is being used more. But to a Russian like myself, the word "body" seems more meaningful and understandable than that of "people of God." "Body" and *sobornost* go better together.

Our unity must be extraordinary. We cannot go about facing catastrophes, which we will, if we are not united. In times of discouragement, it seems that building Christian unity is impossible, and yet I know that God cannot ask the impossible. This desire for unity is so deep in the heart of Christ that we can't stop trying, even though there seems to be a wide gap between the ideal God is calling us to and what seems attainable.

Chapter 12

The Sacraments

His mother said to the servants,
"Do whatever he tells you."
John 2:5

I could learn much about God through study, books and other tools of the mind. But there is a difference between knowing about God and knowing God. Only those to whom he reveals himself know him. This brings us back again to prayer and the sacraments.

It is through prayer and the sacraments that we make a vital contact with Jesus Christ, the Father, and the Holy Spirit. Only then, it seems to me, can we go forth to others, to all humanity, and recognize God in them.

It is astonishing how little we appreciate the Mass and the sacraments. In some current religious literature, one reads that the best way to encounter Christ is in and through another human being. There is seemingly an associated implication that personal approach to Christ in the sacraments and other ways is obsolete. Here the question becomes acute: How can I find Christ in my brother if I do not know him personally first? It seems to me that I cannot recognize him in others if I do not first meet him personally.

What do I mean by this personal meeting? Perhaps I mean the very essence of the mystery of our faith. He gave us two commandments: to love God, and to love our neighbour. (Matthew 22:37–39) In that order! How do I get to know him so that I can love him and continue to love him in my brothers, and to love my brothers because I love him?

I know him because I was baptized into his death and resurrection, and because he knew me first. I know him in the breaking of the Bread. I know him in the sacrament of repentance (which Russians call "the kiss of Christ") when I kneel in sorrow, in confession. I know him in prayer, prayer of all kinds, especially in the prayer of silence.

> The Church herself—as the Second Vatican Council teaches—is "a kind of sacrament or sign of intimate union with God, and of the unity of all mankind."
>
> Pope John Paul II
> To the Youth of the World

It is through prayer and the sacraments that we get to know God. This seems to me to be of the essence. All the rest seems peripheral, like a moth flying around a flame. How can we love others if we do not love God first? How can we love God first, if we do not seek to know him, to meet him as a person? How can we possibly recognize him in others if we have never met him?

In the inner silence of my own heart, he comes with his own intense silence. There he breaks open my heart, quiets the noise, and inspires me to say, "Speak, Yahweh; for your servant is listening." (1 Samuel 3:10)

The Liturgy is a sea of fire into which we plunge and come out burning.

The Liturgy—the Mass—is the most personal, intimate declaration of love that God makes to each of us. In the Eucharist, we can sense his passionate desire to become one with us so that we might live his divine life more abundantly. Christ re-opened the gates of Paradise to us again.

Just think for one moment what happens when you receive in the Eucharist the bread and wine that are the Body and Blood of Christ. You stand in line, you receive the bread and the wine, and, in that moment, God and you are one. The oneness remains, but at this particular moment the oneness is like a flaming fire. That is why when I approach communion I feel an inner trembling and have goose flesh, because of the incredible mercy of God. God and I, through a small piece of bread and a sip of wine, become one.

The scriptures and the liturgy place upon our lips words that give profound expression to our longing. "For my flesh," Christ says to us, "is real food and my blood is real drink. Whoever eats my flesh and drinks my blood lives in me and I live in that person. As the living Father sent me and I draw life from the Father, so whoever eats me will also draw life from me." (John 6:55–57) To eat his flesh, to drink his blood, to absorb into ourselves the living God is beyond any wish we might be capable of forming for ourselves. Yet, it satisfies to the full what we of necessity long for.

Catholics go to church and receive the Body and Blood of Christ, but often forget the words of St. Paul, "Anyone who eats the bread or drinks the cup of the Lord unworthily is answerable for the body and blood of the Lord. Everyone is to examine himself and only then eat of the bread and drink from the cup; because a person who eats and drinks without recognizing the body is eating and drinking his own condemnation." (1 Corinthians 11:27–29)

A Psalm says, "My heart and my flesh thirst for the living God." (Psalm 63:1) Have you really, honestly, been thirsting for the living God? So that there's nothing left, only emptiness? Only when our whole being is joined to his shall we be at rest.

But the question is, have we got any longing? Are we really waking up in the morning and saying, "Today God and I will be one"? Is that love or longing also like a fire? We are looking for God, and his one desire is to become united with us.

The person who participates in the Eucharistic Sacrifice, having been brought there by someone else, will know what love is. He will never hunger again. He will understand, in an incredible way, how much he is loved.

When a person knows that God loves him, he will cease to hunger. He will know that God has prepared a table for him and has invited him to come to his feast, to drink his wine, and to eat the bread which is himself.

Every baptized Christian is called to be a proclaimer of the gospel, through ordinary, nitty-gritty life. We are prophets if we allow the fire of Christ that burns within us to spread through the ordinariness of our daily lives. The Liturgy is the center of our life, a sea of love, a sea of fire into which we plunge and come out burning, ourselves a fire, ready to light fires of love even in the most wretched situations of our day. Yes, liturgy and scripture are the life of our soul.

You died and were born again.

Our Baptism is our real birthday. We are made one with God.

From the *Catechism of the Catholic Church*, "The Sacrament of Baptism" (1218–1228):

> Since the beginning of the world, water, so humble and wonderful a creature, has been the source of life and fruitfulness. Sacred Scripture sees it as 'overshadowed' by the Spirit of God: *At the very dawn of creation your Spirit breathed on the waters, making them the wellspring of all holiness....*
> The Church has seen in Noah's ark a prefiguring of salvation by Baptism, for...'a few...were saved through water': *The waters of the great flood you made a sign of the waters of Baptism, that make an end of sin and a new beginning of goodness.*
> If water springing up from the earth symbolizes life, the water of the sea is a symbol of death and so can represent the mystery of the cross. By this symbolism, Baptism signifies communion with Christ's death.
> But above all, the crossing of the Red Sea, literally the liberation of Israel from the slavery of Egypt, announces the liberation wrought by Baptism: *You freed the children of Abraham from the slavery of Pharaoh, bringing them dry-shod through the waters of the Red Sea, to be an image of the people set free in Baptism.*
> Finally, Baptism is prefigured in the crossing of the Jordan River by which the People of God received the gift of the land promised to Abraham's descendants, an image of eternal life. The promise of this blessed inheritance is fulfilled in the New Covenant....
> All the Old Covenant prefigurations find their fulfillment in Christ Jesus. He begins his public life after having himself baptized by St. John the Baptist in the Jordan. After his resurrection, Christ gives this mission to his apostles: 'Go therefore and make disciples of all nations, baptizing them in the name of the Father and of the Son and of the Holy Spirit, teaching them to observe all that I have commanded you.'...
> The baptized have 'put on Christ.' Through the Holy Spirit, Baptism is a bath that purifies, justifies, and sanctifies.

Hence Baptism is a bath of water in which the 'imperishable seed' of the Word of God produces its life-giving effect.

In the sacrament of Baptism water becomes a love letter from Christ to the person being baptized. What boundless love!

From *The Jerusalem Catecheses:*

You were led to the font of Baptism and…you were immersed in the water…. In (that) instant you died and were born again; the saving water was both your tomb and your mother. Solomon spoke of 'a time to give birth, and a time to die.' For you, however, it was the reverse: a time to die, and a time to be born, although in fact both events took place at the same time and your birth was simultaneous with your death.

This is something amazing and unheard of! It was not we who actually died, were buried and rose again. We only did these things symbolically, but we have been saved in actual fact. It is Christ who was crucified, who was buried and who rose again, yet all this is attributed to us. We share in his sufferings symbolically, and gain salvation in reality!

What boundless love! Christ's undefiled hands were pierced by the nails; he suffered the pain. I experience no pain, no anguish, yet by the share that I have in his sufferings he freely grants me salvation.

We need the light, our Lord Jesus Christ, who is passionate charity, who wedded himself to us through his incarnation, death, and resurrection, and through our Baptism in him. Mary, the Mother of God, is the gate to him who is the light of the world. She is the crossroads of destiny for people today.

One drop of Christ's blood can wash a world clean.

Because sinning means forgetting God, repentance means a turning around, doing what I know I must do. Repentance is the incarnation of the gospel in a person's life. To repent is to change, it is not just to acknowledge that I have done wrong. It is to turn my back to the wrong and start doing right, incarnating the gospel.

Repentance is not remorse. It is not admitting mistakes. It is not saying in self-condemnation, "I've been a fool." Who of us has not recited such a dismal litany? All of us have. Repentance is even more than being sorry for one's sins. It is a moral and spiritual revolution. To repent is one of the hardest things in the world, yet it is basic to all spiritual progress.

Repentance calls for a complete breakdown of pride, of self-assurance, of prestige that comes from success, of the innermost citadel of self-will.

For Catholics, the channel to a return to grace is normally the sacrament of confession or Reconciliation. We go to the man God has appointed, and confess our sins. To me, in my deep faith, any priest is Christ when he is exercising his powers. I kneel before him, but it is not him; in my mind it is Christ. When I kneel and confess my sins and ask forgiveness, Christ in the priest says, "I absolve you of your sin, and grant you pardon and peace," and then I know that I have been made clean.

I have to do some penance, it stands to reason. But the unforgettable thought remains: God so loved the world that he sent his Son into our midst, and at the price of great suffering, his Son reconciled us with God. Because he did so, joy springs forth. The forgiveness of God, the most holy Trinity, covers you.

From the *Catechism of the Catholic Church,* "The Sacrament of Penance and Reconciliation" (1423–1424):

> It is called the *sacrament of conversion* because it makes sacramentally present Jesus' call to conversion, the first step in returning to the Father from whom one has strayed by sin.
>
> It is called the *sacrament of Penance,* since it consecrates the Christian sinner's personal and ecclesial steps of conversion, penance, and satisfaction.
>
> It is called the *sacrament of confession,* since the disclosure or confession of sins to a priest is an essential element of this sacrament. In a profound sense, it is also a 'confession'—acknowledgment and praise—of the holiness of God and of his mercy toward sinful man.
>
> It is called the *sacrament of forgiveness,* since by the priest's sacramental absolution God grants the penitent 'pardon and peace.'
>
> It is called the *sacrament of Reconciliation,* because it imparts to the sinner the love of God who reconciles: 'Be reconciled to God.' He who lives by God's merciful love is ready to respond to the Lord's call: 'Go; first be reconciled to your brother.'

Only love could devise the sacrament of Reconciliation, in which we repent and confess our sins to a priest. Through him we are washed clean. It is as if we are at the foot of Christ's cross and a drop of his precious blood falls on us; one drop can wash a world clean, and it is ours for the asking. His mercy knows no end.

I know Christ through the Holy Spirit who abides with me always.

I know Christ through the Holy Spirit who came to me in his immense power at Confirmation, and who abides with me always.

From the *Catechism of the Catholic Church,* "The Sacrament of Confirmation" (1286–1289, 1319):

> In the Old Testament the prophets announced that the Spirit of the Lord would rest on the hoped-for Messiah for his saving mission. The descent of the Holy Spirit on Jesus at his baptism by John was the sign that this was he who was to come, the Messiah, the Son of God. He was conceived of the Holy Spirit; his whole life and his whole mission are carried out in total communion with the Holy Spirit whom the Father gives him 'without measure.'
> This fullness of the Spirit was not to remain uniquely the Messiah's, but was to be communicated to the whole messianic People....Filled with the Holy Spirit the apostles began to proclaim 'the mighty works of God,' and Peter declared this outpouring of the Spirit to be the sign of the messianic age. Those who believed in the apostolic preaching and were baptized received the gift of the Holy Spirit in their turn.
> From that time on the apostles, in fulfillment of Christ's will, imparted to the newly baptized by the laying on of hands the gift of the Spirit that completes the grace of Baptism....
> Very early, the better to signify the gift of the Holy Spirit, an anointing with perfumed oil (chrism) was added to the laying on of hands. This anointing highlights the name "Christian," which means "anointed" and derives from that of Christ himself whom God "anointed with the Holy Spirit." ...The Eastern Churches call this sacrament Chrismation.... In the West, the term Confirmation suggests that this sacrament both confirms Baptism and strengthens baptismal grace....
> A candidate for Confirmation...must...be prepared to assume the role of disciple and witness to Christ, both within the ecclesial community and in temporal affairs.

"I thirst!"

In the sacrament of Ordination, of Priesthood, Christ who multiplied loaves and fishes to feed us when he walked the earth, has multiplied himself because of love for us. Each priest is another Christ, ordained to feed us with God's word and with his Body and Blood under the form of bread and wine; to preach God's truth; to conduct spiritual direction; to bind and unbind; to dispense his sacraments; to be a guide to lead souls to Christ who thirsts for them, to lead them to the heart of Christ. *"Sitio!"* he says—"I thirst!" (John 19:28)

No one is more relevant than a priest who understands his role as the servant of the Word, as one who can give us God under the form of bread and wine.

From the *Catechism of the Catholic Church,* "The Sacrament of Holy Orders" (1583, 1585–1586):

> The vocation and mission received on the day of his ordination mark him permanently....
> The grace of the Holy Spirit proper to this sacrament is configuration to Christ as Priest, Teacher, and Pastor, of whom the ordained is made a minister.
> For the bishop, this is first of all a grace of strength...the grace to guide and defend his Church with strength and prudence as a father and pastor, with gratuitous love for all and a preferential love for the poor, the sick, and the needy. This grace impels him to proclaim the Gospel to all, to be the model for his flock, to go before it on the way of sanctification by identifying himself in the Eucharist with Christ the priest and victim, not fearing to give his life for his sheep....

St. John Vianney, the holy Curé of Ars, says: "The priest continues the work of redemption on earth.... If we really understood the priest on earth, we would die not of fright but of love.... The Priesthood is the love of the heart of Jesus."

You will know love, because it will be accompanied by pain.

Whenever a man and woman who desire to love him through one another are wedded in the sacrament of Marriage, Christ returns and sits as at the feast of Cana. For all their married life, Christ stands ready, if they ask him, through his Mother or directly, to change the bitter waters of life into the sweet wine of his love, his mercy, and his graces.

Love is always synonymous with sacrifice. Wherever there is love, there is pain. Without sacrifice love is only earthly flaming passion that dies before it is born. Falling in love and marrying need to be done carefully, prayerfully, not limited to whether she or he is physically attractive. You will know love, because it will be accompanied by pain.

Marriage is a vocation, a call of God to two people to become one; to found a home, beget, bear, and raise children; in this glorious and hard vocation, to become saints themselves; and to do all that is in their power to make saints of their children. In marriage, two people enter the most glorious adventure that man and woman can enter, provided they love each other, provided the foundation of their coming together is not lust.

Seeing Christ in each other, they are called to love each other with a great love—a love of service and sacrifice, given joyfully, instantly, at all times, hard and easy. This will demand humility, the fertile soil of their souls, which must be cultivated constantly in order that faith, hope, and charity grow. For without these virtues their marriage will wither before it has time to bring forth its first bud.

From the *Catechism of the Catholic Church,* "The Sacrament of Matrimony" (1602–1605):

> Sacred Scripture begins with the creation of man and woman in the image and likeness of God and concludes with a vision of 'the wedding-feast of the Lamb.'...
> 'The intimate community of life and love which constitutes the married state has been established by the Creator and endowed by him with its own proper laws....God himself is the author of marriage.' The vocation to marriage is written in the very nature of man and woman as they came from the hand of the Creator.
> God who created man out of love also calls him to love—the fundamental and innate vocation of every human being. For man is created in the image and likeness of God who is himself love. Since God created him man and woman, their mutual love becomes an image of the absolute and unfailing love with which God loves man. It is good, very

good, in the Creator's eyes. And this love which God blesses is intended to be fruitful and to be realized in the common work of watching over creation: 'And God blessed them, and God said to them: "Be fruitful and multiply, and fill the earth and subdue it."'

Holy Scripture affirms that man and woman were created for one another: 'It is not good that the man should be alone.' The woman, 'flesh of his flesh,' his equal, his nearest in all things, is given to him by God as a "helpmate"; she thus represents God from whom comes our help. 'Therefore a man leaves his father and his mother and cleaves to his wife, and they become one flesh.' The Lord himself shows that this signifies an unbreakable union of their two lives by recalling what the plan of the Creator had been 'in the beginning': 'So they are no longer two, but one flesh.'

What is lacking in the relationship between men and women today is depth. The common attitude is, what can I get from the other person, instead of what can I give. Even in giving, there is misunderstanding. We think that if we enter into a union with another we are God's gift to them. We are, but only when we think first of the other person, and not of ourselves. If a young person enters into the holy vocation of matrimony "to be loved," and both partners have the same idea, then who is going to do the loving?

Both psychological and Christian maturity is needed; the two complement each other. The sexual attraction between men and women is very strong. Many do not know how to handle themselves.

North American people have sex on the brain. It surrounds us to a tragic degree through television, secularism, and materialism. The worship of sex is reaching the proportions of idolatry. Allied vices accompany it: drunkenness, drugs, abortion, emotional disturbances. A sad spectacle to behold on an overall picture.

Christ gently bends to his Church in distress and calls some of its members to remedy this idolatry through living chaste and celibate lives. To a world drunk with immorality and all its appendages, he evidently wants to show the face of chastity, especially through youth dedicated to his love and his commandments.

All who are not married are called to live chastely, in celibacy. To be faithful in this we need to keep ourselves aware of the physical and emotional differences between men and women, and realize that the nature of a man tends toward sexual union long before he may be aware of it. In a sense, his body is ahead of his conscious self.

We need to be watchful, and think seriously and deeply in situations of relationships with the opposite sex, for in many ways we have forgotten what chastity is all about. To everyone this teaching of Christ was directed: Whoever looks at a person of the opposite sex lustfully has already committed adultery in his or her heart. (Matthew 5:28)

There is so much talk about love, so much experimenting, and so much disappointment with what we imagine love to be. Yet, deep down in our hearts we know that Christ's way of loving is the way of the cross, that it is painful, and that it demands an emptying of ourselves. Without his loving us, none of us could love the way he wants us to.

Christ put the whole matter of chastity in the context of the heart, not of the mind. You and I can spend days and weeks and months rationalizing things away, but the gospel doesn't rationalize. The gospel goes straight to the heart of the matter. Chastity demands purity of heart, for the pure shall see God. (Matthew 5:8) When you see God, your respect and love for your neighbour begins to become like that of the heart of Christ.

We are called to see God in everyone. Once I see God in others, I respect them, I love them. I will not use that person for my own end, that is, that I might be satisfied physically or emotionally—and then drop the person like a rag doll when I am through fulfilling my needs.

Deep and profound are God's words on chastity, and a chaste life has fantastic heights and depths. Jesus Christ came on earth, but he did not marry. Christ himself was celibate and chaste. He set up a pattern, an ideal.

There are people who are chaste in marriage, and there are others who are chaste in celibacy for the kingdom of God. It is God who calls people to the consecrated life, to celibacy. This is a definite vocation.

We see through studying people of ancient pagan cultures that from time immemorial the calling to virginity and respect for it have been inborn in the human race. Today chastity is widely ridiculed, yet humanity continues to respect those who embrace the state of consecrated celibacy. When we see a chaste person, something happens to us, something that we cannot explain. We think of God. Such people are like signposts toward the *parousia,* the second coming of the Lord.

Chastity is like a foretaste of heaven where the saints love one another as Christians. Chastity is a tremendous light which enlightens and warms people. Lay men, women, and priests can all love one another deeply in a wholesome and holy way. But it involves, among other things, becoming aware of how differently men and women react in body, mind, and emotions to a chaste, deep, holy love-friendship being advocated. A chaste beautiful love, within the context of marriage or of consecrated life, is certainly possible for those called to it.

Our earthly pilgrimage is directed toward one goal—union with God.

Then there is the sacrament of the Sick, in which Christ through the priest comes to anoint you. When it is given to those who truly lie in the shadow of death, then Christ in the priest comes to anoint them and to feed them with his Body, in Viaticum, in preparation for the journey ahead. We need to remember, though, that this is not only a sacrament for those who are dying, it is the sacrament of the living. Many who have received it give witness to Christ's miracles of healing, as in days of yore.

From the *Catechism of the Catholic Church:* "The Anointing of the Sick" (1506–1509):

> Christ invites his disciples to follow him by taking up their cross in their turn. By following him they acquire a new outlook on illness and the sick. Jesus associates them with his own life of poverty and service. He makes them share in his ministry of compassion and healing: 'So they went out and preached that men should repent. And they cast out many demons, and anointed with oil many that were sick and healed them.'
>
> The risen Lord renews this mission ('In my name . . . they will lay their hands on the sick, and they will recover.') and confirms it through the signs that the Church performs by invoking his name. These signs demonstrate in a special way that Jesus is truly 'God who saves.'
>
> The Holy Spirit gives to some a special charism of healing so as to make manifest the power of the grace of the risen Lord. But even the

most intense prayers do not always obtain the healing of all illnesses. Thus St. Paul must learn from the Lord that 'my grace is sufficient for you, for my power is made perfect in weakness,' and that the sufferings to be endured can mean that 'in my flesh I complete what is lacking in Christ's afflictions for the sake of his Body, that is, the Church.'

'Heal the sick!' The Church has received this charge from the Lord and strives to carry it out by taking care of the sick as well as by accompanying them with her prayer of intercession. She believes in the life-giving presence of Christ, the physician of souls and bodies.

Many Christians are fearful and grim about death, as if they were not believers in Christ. Death is awesome, there is no denying that, for it is the cessation of being as we know it through our experience. It's normal to mourn the death of those dear to us, for we lose their immediate presence. But, today, we Catholics are so divorced from our Christian sources that we fear even the thought of death. Of course, others capitalize on our fears since our non-Christian attitude to death is flourishing.

Behind the fear and gloom is the idea of the just punishment that God meted out to Adam and Eve for original sin. We are aware of that, but we have forgotten that Christ conquered death, and that from the moment of his resurrection, death has lost its sting. (1 Corinthians 15:54–57) Death is a most awesome moment between lives. We enter into a new life, the life of love, the life of union with God, of happiness and joy, there to wait until the *parousia*. In the Church's liturgical calendar of saints, it is the day of death which is celebrated. It is considered to be the saints' birthday in the Lord.

Because our faith in Christ's redemption of us is so weak, we push aside the thought of death, rather than preparing for it. Heaven is a state of union with God of such joy and happiness that St. Paul says, "What no eye has seen and no ear has heard, what the mind of man cannot visualize; all that God has prepared for those who love him." (1 Corinthians 2:9) Our earthly pilgrimage, not only ours personally but that of the whole servant, pilgrim Church, is directed toward this one goal of union with God.

Chapter 13

Stewardship

*Words flow out of what fills the heart.
Good people draw good things from their store of goodness;
bad people draw bad things from their store of badness.*

Matthew 12:34-35

Once we are baptized into the life and death of Jesus Christ, we receive a tremendous call to stewardship; we receive the keys of his kingdom. It is up to us to open its doors and to find out all about it. We are called to penetrate every corner of this kingdom of ours because we are stewards of it. We have entered into it, not for ourselves alone, but for the whole world. For Christ says, "Go out to the whole world; proclaim the gospel to all creation." (Mark 16:15)

Christ often spoke of stewardship, once very powerfully in his parable of the talents. (Matthew 25:14–30) When we search the gospel we realize the immensity of stewardship. Our stewardship begins with baptism, with becoming members of Christ's body. It includes stewardship of the Word.

As I become the steward of my heart, I open the door of God's kingdom to others.

There is the stewardship of the heart—my heart. I use the talents that God has given me to penetrate deeply into his laws: "Master, which is the greatest commandment?" Jesus replies, "You must love the Lord your God with all your heart, with all your soul, and with all your mind....The second resembles it: You must love your neighbour as yourself." (Matthew 22:37–39)

What a tremendous stewardship, because as I become the steward of my heart in order to grow in God's law of love, I become like him. Then, I open the door of his kingdom to others through my example.

I am responsible.

From its cosmic and dynamic immensity stewardship comes slowly down to the nitty-gritty everydayness of our life. I am responsible for so many things; the pollution of the earth begins with me. Do I use sprays that change the stratosphere?

In feeding the people under my care am I alert to unhealthy chemicals? Here my stewardship can fall into literally small pieces or nonexistence, because I do not read, do not listen; I do not inform myself. Consequently, I feed my brothers and sisters things that hurt them. Then, I hear the words of Christ saying, "Take the talent from him and give it to the man who has five talents. For to everyone who has, more will be given, but from the man who has not, even what he has will be taken away." (Matthew 25:29)

I am responsible for my part of everything.

Stewardship becomes narrower and deeper. I am the steward of everything that I use: utensils in the kitchen, books in the library, computer files, furniture, tools. Everything has to be kept in order, no matter how shabby or poor. Exterior order is the sign of interior order. I am steward of things which need to be repaired.

This kind of stewardship goes very deep. It demands a tremendous inner discipline. Yes, stewardship pertains to everything, and I am responsible for my part of that everything.

I am responsible for how I care for my neighbour.

But no sooner does stewardship go into details of cluttered rooms, dirty kitchens, messes of all sorts, than it soars upwards where we become stewards also of our brothers and sisters, of our neighbour.

This means stewardship of my speech, of my attention, of my emotions, of my thoughts. It goes through my heart into my subconscious. Suppose one of the members of our family talks to me and my mind wanders and it becomes rather obvious in my face and my eyes that I am not listening. Stewardship is broken, and the Lord will demand an accounting of it. Suppose I pass on some gossip, something detrimental to someone. Stewardship of the tongue is a deep spiritual discipline that has to be prayed for constantly.

When someone is given a great deal, a great deal will be demanded of that person; when someone is entrusted with a great deal, of that person even more will be expected.

Luke 12:48

I am expected to spend wisely the gifts of God.

So we have started with baptism, in which we die and resurrect with Christ. How dynamic stewardship is, how high it soars, and how simple it can become at the base, only to return to heights again. As in the parable, we are expected to spend wisely this "money" of his, which is love, understanding, and especially unselfishness.

Stewardship is a little thing such as washing well some dishes, and it is as immense as the heart of man uniting itself with the heart of God who is steward of the universe.

Chapter 14

Living with Danger

> To you my friends I say: Do not be afraid
> of those who kill the body and after that can do no more.
>
> Luke 12:4

At times of national emergencies we seem to live in a suspended moment of time. It is a breathless, fearsome, and tragic moment. Our fears are legitimate, not illusory. But we need to be prepared for these moments. We need to remember that we belong to God who is perfect love and that perfect love casts out all fears or makes them bearable through his grace. (1 John 4:18)

The first step in such emergencies is to gather in prayer, prayer for peace, prayer for the dark clouds to pass by, prayer for people to keep their sanity, prayer that people remember that God exists. Then, we ought to continue our prayer individually for the same ends, calling on the mercy of God and beseeching his intervention in our human affairs.

Those of us who are far removed from the seat of the conflict at the time must then go about our business, which is the business of God, just as before the crisis. The greatest contribution that we can give or make at that moment is to go about our duty of the moment and offer it up for the same intentions as our prayers. (1 Peter 4:7) At no time ought we Christians to show panic in the face of destruction and death. Let us bring God's peace into the troubled and frightened hearts of others.

There are real dangers to be faced—prepare to face them with courage.

Feeling fear in the face of real danger is appropriate. In the face of imminent danger, we experience psychosomatic reactions, the normal result of rational fears. Our self-preservation tendencies are aroused. This is perfectly normal.

The simple thing to do is to discuss our fears openly with each other and pray to God for courage. Do not let shame lead you to hide your fears from one another. Be open and simple and talk about these things without shame.

Courage is not the absence of fear; on the contrary, if you were not afraid, you could not be courageous. Courage lies in overcoming fear because of a motivation—love of family, love of country, but most of all because of faith in God. Our courage finds its source and life in God and arises out of deep faith in him. We Christians are called to give courage to others.

Now is the crucial time to accept that there are real dangers to be faced and to prepare to face them with courage. While being courageous may mean standing still and overcoming your fear, it may also mean running away. Virtue does not lie in being without fear or in being able to withstand your opponent through a show of your own strength, but in trusting God that, at the moment of disaster, immense and special graces will be given to you.

Let our voices remain calm and quiet, our steps unhurried, our schedules ordinary; let our homes be refuges of peace and calm.

Nevertheless, we need to take all precautions necessary to prolong our lives and those of others. Our thoughts must be of peace and of love for the other person, not of ourselves. We can give peace to those who are so emotionally fearful that they can't think straight.

We need to be prepared for such emergencies. Let us stand ready to be of any assistance to our governments in the way of helping with the organization of First Aid, feeding stations, or in whatever ways we are capable. Let us be ready to serve God and neighbour without counting the cost.

Let us never pass on rumours that are unconfirmed. Let us be quenchers of rumours, rather than spreading them. Let us be truthful without exaggerating, and if need be, discuss only official information. Let our voices be always calm and quiet, our steps unhurried, and the ordinary schedule of the day kept unchanged whenever possible. Let our homes be refuges of peace and calm.

Whatever we do in public or in private, let us be efficient, peaceful and quiet, in the way we talk and walk, in our posture and in our voices. Let us be men and women of constant prayer. If possible let us keep in touch with our loved ones, and if not possible let us commend each other and ourselves to God in peace, faith, confidence, and hope, because of his love for us and our love for him who is Lord of life and death.

Let us be gathered together like sheep around our Shepherd, Jesus Christ. Let us be one before the Lord—of one mind, one heart, totally one with him. Right now, the sheep need to be around the Shepherd and take on his thoughts, his mind. We need to be friends with one another, to be one in Christ. We are never going to be one if we are afraid; we have to overcome fear with faith and love.

Let us pray.

Strip yourself by your own free choice.

To travel across America is to face the possibility of bombs, knives, revolvers, all kinds of arms. Vandalism is rampant. No matter where you turn, human life is cheap, and terror reigns in the hearts of many. There is the feeling that something is going to happen, though nobody can tell when.

Our preparation for that tragic and chaotic situation also calls us to change our habits of life-style, to stop being bourgeois, to get rid of quite a bit, to live simply. Tomorrow we may be stripped of everything. This is the time of stripping myself by my own free choice, the time of facing that the world is in chaos, because it has denied God.

Live by a profound, unalterable faith that whatever happens, happens with God's permission.

We also have to live by a profound, unalterable faith that whatever happens, happens with God's permission. Whenever you have an obstacle, face it directly. If the truth is on your side, so is Christ, and sooner or later he will show you what he wants in the situation.

We've got to face the fact that our duty will be to preach the gospel with our lives, no matter what. Constantly, irrevocably, totally, for our dedication must be total. To prepare now to preach the gospel with our lives, we have to enter a period of prayer and fasting—before the tragedy.

We need to be patient, and to forgive. We are called to open our hearts to those who are creating all the horrors that are being produced. We may be engulfed in the horror and all we will be able to do is to be as Christ was—meek as a lamb being led to the slaughter. (Isaiah 50:5–8) God will give us strength to endure it. The greatest witness one can give to God is martyrdom.

Chapter 15

Overcoming Fear

*There is no need to be afraid, little flock,
for it has pleased your Father to give you the kingdom.*

Luke 12:32

Many people walk around in fear—psychological fear, spiritual fear, intellectual fear. We look around and hear on all sides the explosion of bombs. We go to sleep wondering if our cities will be attacked. People are afraid to travel by air, and even by train or other means of transportation. There is constantly the fear of something going wrong.

What about all those terrorists? The world is full of them, and nobody seems to be able to stop them. Italy, France, England, Ireland, Germany, U.S.A., everywhere and anywhere there are terrorists who bring terror into the hearts of men.

Courage is not the absence of fear, but fear overcome by faith. How can we doubt that our life is glorious when it is God who has called us to this life?

Love one another.

Fear is certainly a weapon of Satan, one way or another. Fears take people away from God and create tragedy upon tragedy. I cry out to God the Father to take away our fears, especially from the young who are struggling to live the Christian life, the gospel without compromise.

Fear is exorcised by two things: one is prayer and the other is forgiveness of those who have done us harm. And the first person that we need to forgive is ourselves.

God told us to love one another. It is essential for us to be convinced that love alone can bring about the salvation of the world. Let us begin to love. Let us turn our face to God. Let us simply take it for granted that we will share with those who haven't got what we have or who are in greater need. Let us begin to live the gospel without compromise, and fear will be cast out. Love will come to reign, and we might yet experience its fruit: peace. Our fallout shelters might yet become simple storage rooms, or, better yet, children's playrooms. Places of life and not strongholds against death.

To be a Christian is to risk everything including your life.

Fear puts deep and tragic roots into a person's heart. With fear comes doubt. Look at all the bombings and destructions. How can I believe in a God who would permit such things? Extreme doubt, like a poisonous flower, comes forth.

No one remembers that his God is tender, compassionate, understanding, forgiving. Nobody stops to think that God did not start the bombing, did not hijack the planes, did not kill or maim people in wars. There is a strange aggressiveness in us which blames God for these things. Perhaps it is begotten by the doubts, the fear, the near-madness that surrounds us today on all sides.

To be a Christian is to risk everything including your life. Nothing may be held back. It is to enter a no-man's land, where you are ridiculed, rejected, misunderstood, maligned, persecuted. You have to walk in Christ's footsteps there. Because you love him, nothing will make you deviate from following those footsteps.

We are afraid of risk. This is why the world today shies away from commitment, even commitment to God's authority. Marriage, religious life, all are viewed as only temporary, but with God there is nothing temporary. With God it's all or nothing at all. Christ said, "If anyone declares himself for me in the presence of human beings, I will declare myself for him in the presence of my Father." (Matthew 10:32) He also said, "Anyone who is not with me is against me." (Matthew 12:30)

When the cross is heavy, well, I just keep on walking. If God has sent it to me, he will give me strength to go on with it. It helps to divide the day into hours.

Be a fool.

Most people are terribly afraid to express themselves lest they be ridiculed. Ridicule makes them shut up and go inside of themselves. They sit there and look to the left and to the right, saying to themselves, "What is he or she thinking about what I say?" Why are we so afraid of being ridiculed? Christ said to St. Francis, "Be a fool the like of which has never been seen." We may be rejected or not approved of. To be a fool for Christ is to expose yourself to ridicule.

If we do not put our roots in Christ, we only survive clippety-clop. We follow the crowd. We are afraid to stand out, but God wants us to stand out. "Whoever is not with me is against me." To be with him is to stand out of the crowd. It is to be subject to ridicule. It is to be different, to have a different attitude toward our worth. It's to relate our worth not to what we have produced but to Christ's death on the cross for each of us. It's to be God-minded, God-saved, God-rescued people.

Stand still and listen.

Over the whole world, whether we know it or not, the strange pall of sin falls like a dark fog, and we are walking through it. No wonder we are full of fears.

"No one can have greater love than to lay down his life for his friends." (John 15:13) "Perfect love drives out fear." (1 John 4:18) Perfect love lays down its life. Have we forgotten about this? It seems we have.

We had better remember before it is too late, and before fear has bound us with its strong and ominous ropes—before we really die the death of our souls. If we allow fear to dominate us, then, indeed, those who have the power to kill our bodies will also have the power to kill our souls, and we shall have given them that power.

We stand on a very narrow edge today. Which way are we going to move? Along the edge of faith, hope, and love? This is the path God gives us when we listen. On either side is an abyss. Which are we going to choose? It's up to us. This is the hour of choosing. May it be the hour of standing still, the hour of listening, the hour of prayer.

Freedom is achieved by prayer. Only some kind of contact with God will make us free. Prayer is sometimes such a hard thing.

Stand still and listen, and God will blow away the fog if we let him.

Chapter 16

Nonviolence

*If anyone hits you on the right cheek, offer him the other as well;
if someone wishes to go to law with you to get your tunic,
let him have your cloak as well.
And if anyone requires you to go one mile, go two miles with him....
Love your enemies and pray for those who persecute you,
so that you may be children of your Father in heaven,
for he causes his sun to rise on the bad as well as the good,
and sends down rain to fall on the upright and the wicked alike.*

Matthew 5:39-41, 44-45

Much has been said about nonviolence. Young people of the campus world and people in all walks of life have talked of it. Certainly the examples of Gandhi and Martin Luther King—one a Hindu and the other a Christian—served to focus the interest of the world on this deeply spiritual way of bringing peace to a world filled with hate and violence.

How can one remain nonviolent in the face of hatred, hostility, bodily attacks? Nonviolence does not mean one will stay at home, passive, noncommitted, noninvolved, when confronted with attitudes that endanger both life and sanity. For when we cease to burn with love, then the world will truly turn cold.

To put it another way, true nonviolence has its roots in love, a love that believes that it is called to lay down its very life for the other.

The nonviolent needs to be motivated by a dream, and there can be nothing wishy-washy about that dream. I need to be rooted in faith—faith in a cause, faith in a Person, faith in God.

Without faith, nonviolence is impossible. There will come a moment of choice, a moment of standing at the crossroads of decision. A decision that may well entail life or death. Strange as this may seem, to be nonviolent, to make such decisions, to be ready to lay down one's life both for the other and for one's beliefs, demands violence.

Yes, violence to oneself! For heaven is taken by violence. True nonviolence begins with violence to oneself. (Matthew 11:12) What does violence to oneself mean? It means to be humble, to be poor, to be meek, to be pure of heart, to be empty of self, of selfish motives. It means to have a dream that is dreamed in God. The nonviolent of whom Christ spoke are the pure of heart who will see God. (Matthew 5:8) They are the meek who will inherit the earth. (Matthew 5:4)

The novitiate of preparation and cleansing includes prayer and fasting, as was the practice of Gandhi and King. Only through this kind of novitiate is the ability, the grace, the charism of nonviolence achieved.

Violence to self comes from the Holy Spirit and is gentle and persistent. It urges one to cleanse oneself from everything except love and to create within oneself a climate that will give birth to unconquerable courage. It is this burning with love which alone will enable us to preach nonviolence and to be nonviolent.

Stand up and be counted.

It is good for a Christian to take part in peace and protest marches, but it is utterly against the gospel to turn peace marches into hate marches. Within the Catholic Church, it is good to courageously face authority, whoever that authority may be. But the way to face it is *à la* St. Thomas More, who spoke the truth to kings and prelates without fear. He also did not attempt to escape the consequences of such confrontations, and was martyred. There is another big "also": he did everything in charity.

Here lies the crux of our modern confusion, the almost utter confusion that at present is shaking the minds of young and old alike. How can one be a pacifist if there is no peace in one's heart? How can we heal our neighbours, the "poor rich," the "rich poor," if we have neither the oil of compassion nor the wine of love?

As this involvement of love between us grows and deepens, we enter into a revolution. A revolution in which there is a violence directed only against oneself. There is much to be overcome, so terribly much, before we can say with St. Paul, "I live now, not I, but Christ lives in me." (Galatians 2:20) This kind of warfare truly brings about a revolution in the individual and in the community of mankind. The revolution of Christ brings about a whole new set of values.

The archbishop of Toronto once asked me where I got the courage to stand up against injustices, and I replied, "From Jesus Christ!" So I now say, "Stand up and be counted!" If you are a man or woman, American or Canadian, or of whatever nation, stand up and be counted. You believe in the reality of God, who is the root of all goodness. But it is so easy to have a beer, look at the TV, and forget all the injustices. We are selling our birthright for a mess of pottage. Today, it is very tasty, but tomorrow it won't be.

If you are hit on one cheek, turn the other.

At what point in the hidden depths of a person's heart and soul does just anger begin? At what point does a Christian lift the cords of that anger to chase the moneylenders out of the temple? (John 2:13–17) When does a person reach the breaking point and begin to speak with words of fire and truth to a mighty and powerful one of the world?

There is such a thing as just anger. We see it in the gospel. Christ did pick up cords and chase the moneylenders out of the temple; he did call the Pharisees and Sadducees vipers and whitened sepulchers. (Matthew 23:13–32)

I personally know the terrible storms of anguish when just anger shakes a person like a fever, like a fierce cold wind which makes one's teeth rattle. I knew it in the slums of Toronto during the Depression when long queues of hungry men waited in line in front of the storefront of our Friendship House. We were without food ourselves. Our begging did not bring us anything to share with them. Yet, on the evening of that day, I was invited to lecture to a Catholic audience in a swanky hotel where men and women were eating rich and costly food which they did not need.

I knew it in the Harlems of America where I spent ten years. My one desire there was to have black skin. I traveled across that vast country crying out into indifferent and cold white faces the pain of African-Americans. When I was almost lynched in the South, I was glad. And the tomatoes, eggs and other things that were thrown at me occasionally by some audiences didn't stop me. I didn't care about the open and often hidden persecution to which I was subjected. My just anger was too great for the caring. I prayed that I might die for my African-American brothers and sisters, but God did not grant this.

I cannot deny that I often used words like cords, and that very often, upon returning to my bedbug-infested room in Harlem, the powerful temptation to use my talent for words to arouse the African-Americans to violence would come upon me.

I am still filled with this just anger, because the face of poverty and injustice, the face of man's inhumanity to man, is still before me everywhere I go. It is present in the rural slums of Canada, in the vast North with its Indian minorities, in the "developing" countries.

As I travelled across the U.S.A. and Canada, I saw violence and lack of respect for human life. In a word, I felt that we had returned to a sort of barbarism of past centuries, for people are afraid to walk their own streets.

I, who consider myself an apostle of peace and nonviolence, am shaken. At what point does this just anger, this searing pain which never leaves one, at what point does it cross over an imaginary line and burst into the kind of violence that we see all around us?

Christ's answer is always a paradox. He says, "All who draw the sword will die by the sword" (Matthew 26:52) and, "To anyone who slaps you on one cheek, present the other cheek as well." (Luke 6:29) But, then, he picks up cords to remove animals and moneychangers from the temple. (John 2:13–17) He also uses words as swords.

How long is it possible for a Christian to watch the face of the poor being ground into the dust by the rich? How long is it possible to watch governments of affluent nations dole out mere fistfuls of grain to the hungry when granaries are bursting? How long is it possible to watch people gorge themselves while half of the world is starving? Just anger is a devouring fire in thousands of Christians' hearts and minds.

I have only one answer for myself: unceasing prayer, fasting, and a "yes" to God, to remain crucified on the cross of tense, just anger. I feel safe on that strange wooden cross. He who is nailed to it cannot succumb to the temptation to do violence to others, for temptation it really is. A crucified person can only hang there and slowly die for those with whom he identifies.

Perhaps that is the only answer—suffering on that cross. Such people cannot do anything but die. They die so that hope may be born in the hearts of the poor. They die so that love may blossom in the hearts of the rich, a love that will reach to the very bottom of the poverty of their brethren.

Blessed are the meek.

Nonviolence is connected with meekness. "Blessed are the meek," Christ says. (Matthew 5:4) The person who is meek will advance to proclaim the rights of African-Americans or whoever, without concern for his own life. He speaks the truth as it is, notwithstanding any kind of punishment, possible or actual. For example, I've heard of an Austrian soldier who refused to go into Hitler's army. He simply said, "No," and for this he died.

Meekness can be terrifying to an opponent, since he cannot penetrate it nor get around it. Meekness is edifying by its simplicity. Meekness deals with integrity.

Christian nonviolence is built on basic human unity. We cannot violate the other, even for a high purpose. I can't think of any virtue that so exacts from him who tries to practice it, all his power, all his ability. It takes guts to be meek, guts beyond our ken. And the way to get there is to pray. We don't want to surrender to this idea of meekness and humility. Meekness is a total reliance on God. Meekness is also the absence of anger. But this absence is not won overnight.

Justice without love is bitter, cold, harsh, seldom healing or restoring.

We certainly need to be concerned about world problems—people who are hungry, poor, and victims of injustice. Perhaps the word is not "concerned" but "tormented." We are called to be so concerned, so tormented by the plight of the world that we almost become the other.

How can we identify with humanity in this profound, total manner, or rather incarnate this humanity into ourselves? There is already much involvement and even much real concern. Many speak of justice and seek through all possible means to secure it for themselves and for others.

But in all this concern there is much confusion and chaotic thinking. It seems that many have forgotten that justice is always the child of love. Justice without love is bitter, cold, seldom healing or restoring. Justice without love is often harsh even when it presents real truths.

Love is a Person, love is God. Where God is, there is love. We try to cut God up into pieces, one part being justice and the other, love. In the reality of daily living, we cannot give one without the other.

It is evident these days that we are trying to give justice without love. We try to give truth abstractly as if it only came from books and our minds. In a word, we have divorced our heads from our hearts. How can we bring the two together so that mankind can be given what it needs with a tremendous love, a love which holds justice on the platter of humility, another name for truth? In order to make such a connection, we need to pray.

Chapter 17

Faith

In all truth I tell you, unless a wheat grain falls into the earth and dies, it remains only a single grain; but if it dies it yields a rich harvest. Anyone who loves his life loses it; anyone who hates his life in this world will keep it for eternal life. Whoever serves me, must follow me, and my servant will be with me wherever I am. If anyone serves me, my Father will honour him.

John 12:24-26

Our time in history is one of a rejection of God and his teaching. The word "love" is heard all over the world, but he, the source of all love, Love itself, is being rejected and ignored. Faith is on the wane.

What is faith? Some say they have lost it. Some hunger for the first taste. Some are indifferent to whether they have it or not. Others fight against it, hate it, and want to destroy it in others.

Faith is a free gift from God; no one can really acquire faith by his own efforts.

In a former age of faith, there was no questioning of God's existence. There was a beginning effort to apply his teachings. Social justice, equality, the dignity of persons—all these were on the books, so to speak. They were not fully incarnated, but faith was universal in the Christian world.

How strange that many Christians today seem to miss the greatest point of their faith. God is often seen as "the man with the big stick." The great commandment to love God with all one's heart

(Matthew 22:37) has been turned into a yardstick of implacable justice: "Toe the line or else you'll go to hell."

God's love seems never to have touched the hearts of many religious people. They do not see that the tremendous glad news is that God first loved us. (1 John 4:19) Because of this lack of awareness, because of a fearful attitude toward God, the lives of many Christians are full of fears. They seek remedies for these fears, searching everywhere except where the remedy can be found—in God. If only we all realized that every word he has said and his every commandment leads to true freedom, happiness, peace, and joy—the very things that people are so desperately seeking everywhere.

It is quite clear that the task of every Christian is to be the leaven of the world by bringing this glorious, wondrous, joyful truth to people's hearts. Every baptized person is called to go about the world proclaiming this one truth: God loved us first.

It may help us if we reread what Jesus Christ has said about love. It might help if we meditated on his words and made them our own, made them both the way and the goal of our lives. For he told us first to love God with all our hearts, with all our minds, souls, our whole being, and then to love our neighbour as ourselves, (Matthew 22:37–39) which implies that we first need to learn to love ourselves well. He also said, "By this shall all men know that you are my disciples, that you love one another as I have loved you." (John 13:35) Finally, he said, "Love your enemies." (Luke 6:35)

He defined all the ways of loving. He not only defined them, he lived them. He was Love incarnate, and he showed us in truth that "no one can have greater love than to lay down his life for his friends." (John 15:13)

Jesus spoke these words. But what is more, he incarnated them, dying for us a tortured and painful death. Love has no limits.

Prostrate before him, imploring, crying out for faith.

Faith is a free, loving gift of God to human beings. Faith is the cradle of love and of hope. But this gift given to us at our baptism can grow, must grow, be incarnated into our lives, become part of us, become, like breathing, an utterly integral part of us.

How can faith become all these things? By prayer. God never refuses a prayer for deepening and growth in faith. Prayer is the food that will make faith grow, strengthen it, root it with deep and lasting roots into our hearts.

Faith also grows through living it out.

When I speak of faith, I mean a land of darkness. And, in a manner of speaking, a land of pain. For it is not easy to walk in darkness wondering about the abysses and crevices and pitfalls that might be wide open at our feet. In this year when one can almost hear the world cracking apart, it is not easy to walk in faith, in total belief in the Most Holy Trinity. But God will give us that faith if we continually pray for it.

Always have your answer ready for people who ask you the reason for the hope that you have....Give it with courtesy and respect.

1 Peter 3:15–16

Faith is received on our knees. This is the time when we ought to be prostrate before him, imploring, crying out for faith.

We don't believe in the mystery of ourselves. And that leads us inevitably to lose part of our faith, or maybe all of it. Conversely, to believe in God is to believe in ourselves, for God is in us. When faith envelops us, the two mysteries meet—God and the human person. To love oneself means to live by faith.

Pray while you work and work while you pray.

God has given this day into our hands. This is the day in which we pray, but we pray by action and sweat, just as Christ did. He said he "came not to be served but to serve." (Matthew 20:28) He also said, "Pray continually." (Luke 18:1) Pray while you work and work while you pray.

The duty of the moment is our strategic place. One day at a time. We have this day in which to open our hearts like doors, and take in everyone that we can. Today we have to love as God loved us.

Some feel as if the routine of our daily duties is not enough, that other things should be added. Stop here. Please stop. Fall on your knees and pray and listen. Walk slowly, in the darkness of faith—because you believe in the Trinity, for no other reason. Then, through hope and love, be faithful to your duty of the present moment. That is the essence of Christianity. That is the heart of the Church. The rest flows from it, but this is to come first, walking in faith while doing our daily routine of duties.

It might seem strange but it is the fruit of that faith and hope that the Lord, bending, picks up. With this fruit, he changes the world and allows his Church to expand, because one, two, three, or more people believe, hope, and love.

Our daily work, routine or not, exciting or unexciting, monotonous or not, is part of that faith, hope, and love. This workaday world of ours is the outer shell of a deep inner grace that God gives us. It is because we believe, we hope, and we love that we can do what might seem impossible.

Christ wants us to be an icon of himself, to be people of faith beyond reason, to be fools for God in utter simplicity, and to be people who plead for others in prayer.

Faith demands martyrdom.

We need to ask for faith, not only in God but in other people. Nonbelief is suicidal. Either I enter upon a life of faith in God and others, or I will enter upon a life of despair. There is an enlargement of heart and a pulsating, fantastic fire that comes with faith.

Deep in the heart of faith, this gift of God, lies a marvelous understanding of who we are. Who are we? We are people of the towel and the water. Jesus washed the feet of his apostles with a basin of water and dried them with a towel. (John 13:1–14) Faith will make of us people of the towel and the water. Faith knows no barriers. Faith liberates.

Our contemporary age of faith also demands martyrdom. A strange kind of martyrdom, a white martyrdom—a martyrdom of ridicule by one's peers, by young and old alike. A martyrdom of loneliness. In the *diaspora,* we Christians often have to walk alone amidst uncomprehending crowds. We have to be ready to be not only ridiculed but rejected with contempt.

God extends the invitation to you, he invites you to Gethsemane, there to sweat out your struggle with him, because there will be a struggle. (Matthew 26:36–46) He invites you to stand before the High Priest, that is, before all those of our own faith who will in some way laugh at you, jeer at you, maybe persecute you. (Matthew 26:37–67) Then he invites you to come with him to Pontius Pilate, in that terrible solitude, in that totally strange land that a person enters before dying, that pre-death land. (John 18:28–19:16) Christ will take you by the hand and lead you to Golgotha to be crucified on the other side of his cross. (John 19:17–34) Finally, he will bring you to the joy of his resurrection, which will lead you into a new land where there is no solitude, no silence, no strangeness. (Matthew 28:1–10) There is only a pilgrimage of love toward love.

Sow your faith lavishly into the fields of others' souls, by incarnating it in your life.

This is the age of *diaspora* faith, a faith that is to be lavishly sown into the four winds against all odds, especially against the forces of the intellect. We live in a technological society intoxicated with the exploits of going into outer space and with mechanical gadgets of all kinds. It's a society which demands that everything be measured, weighed, programmed, and put into neat little mental cubbyholes.

In the midst of all this scientific achievement, we are called to sow the seeds of faith into people's souls. In each person, there is still a field, a small knoll, a garden that longs for reseeding. Each person, in their deepest being, does not want to be put into a cubbyhole. We need and want the open spaces where we can be ourselves and breathe. We long especially for the open spaces of the spirit, spaces where God dwells, he for whom we hunger.

This is the age of faith, not so much for those who have never had it, but for those who have lost it, wrapped it up somewhere deep within themselves, buried it so deeply that they have forgotten that they ever had it, or where they have buried it.

It is up to us to tell them by our lives that God is with us. It is for us to be a light to their feet and to help put those feet on the path of rediscovery of faith. (Psalm 119:105) For both them and ourselves this is the path of prayer.

We are called to sow faith by incarnating it in our lives, by living the gospel, by praying and by becoming pilgrims—pilgrims with an eternal lantern in our hands, the lantern and light of Christ.

Pray for faith and to have the heart of a child.

Much of the world is on the defensive. We always have our guards up. We have shields and bucklers and masks not of the Lord's making but of our own, to protect ourselves from real or imagined threats or attacks.

Ours are times of neurosis and psychosis. During the past 400 years or so, many Christians have been drifting away from God until they finally cut themselves off from him officially and completely. At that point, around them and from them begin to stem the fruits of evil—fears, confusion, insecurity. Evil becomes incarnated and spreads in ever-widening circles until even believers are affected in one way or another.

Because of this tragic situation of the world's soul, as it were, all of us are somewhat confused and frightened of threats and attacks, from bombs or even from our next door neighbour. We need to pray for faith (Mark 9:24) and to have the heart of a child, (Matthew 18:2–4) of whom is the kingdom of heaven. When we are anchored in Christ and become like Christ, then from our hearts and souls will stream a light that is from him, and it will illumine and heal the attacker.

Trust is a tender offshoot of faith and is very fragile. Yet, without trust there can be no bonds between husband and wife, between children and parents, between men and women in general. Nor in the world, government to government, peoples to peoples. Because of this lack of trust we have continual wars. How can we have outward peace when there is no inward peace? Inner peace lies in the arms of faith and trust, and of course in love and hope.

We are called to have faith in one another and tenderly nurture the gentle virtue of trust.

Chapter 18

Hope

> He told them a parable about the need to pray continually and never lose heart.... "Will not God see justice done to his elect if they keep calling to him day and night even though he still delays to help them? I promise you, he will see justice done to them, and done speedily.
>
> Luke 17:1, 7-8

It is the end of an era. The world news is such that it seems everything is falling apart, that it is in the throes of evil. My sense is that we are going to be very hard hit. How can we find hope? We are all free to choose good or evil, free to live the gospel or not, to say Yes or No to the Holy Spirit. But no matter what we have done or been, with God every moment is the moment of beginning again. On my window sill is the motto: Expect a miracle. I believe in miracles, and in this case the miracle of prayer and of total, uncompromising surrender to God.

Whatever seems hopeless has within it a potential for light.

A man, the "good thief," was crucified next to Christ, and asked God to take care of him. And Christ said, "Today you will be with me in paradise." (Luke 23:43) Between the speech of the thief and the speech of God, everything began again and an immense, all-embracing hope surged forth.

We who are responsible for the hopelessness of the old, the forgotten, the hungry, are guilty of a terrible sin. Yet whatever seems hopeless has within it a potential for light. Whatever darkness has come upon us, it is passing.

Christ comes to us, and we come out of the tomb of our doubts, fears, and pain.

As we reach middle age and look back on our life, it at times appears to be almost meaningless. We feel that we have nothing to show for it in terms of success, of making good. All we see are mounds of clothing washed or dishes, endless pages of computer work, endless phone calls. They seem like a dreary highway with no one passing by. We doubt our vocation, the wisdom of God that brought us to this point. Doubt surrounds us at times like a London fog.

Or as old age comes upon us we look at our life and we don't find in it anything worth recording. We feel that we have been utter failures. That is the moment to look at Christ's life, which by human standards seemed to "end" in failure.

As we go along the road of our life, feeling at times almost hopeless, we are visited by Christ. (Luke 24:13–35) Somehow or other the resurrected Christ passes through the door of our heart without knocking or opening it. (John 29:19) He comes to us and we, like Lazarus, come out of the tomb of our doubts, fears, and pain. (John 11:41–44)

We are God's children, created to share life with one another. Can we not hold our doubts up against the heart of God and see with the eyes of our soul and heart how many people our lives have touched? Haven't we been called by God to witness by our presence wherever we might be and through whatever we might be doing?

God first, my neighbour second, and myself third.

When I look upon trust today, after a lifetime of experience, I understand better how tremendously difficult its practice is for people who have been brought up in pragmatism. The general idea seems to be to trust no one but oneself and to look after oneself, because no one else will. For many years, I've had a little motto: "God first, my neighbour second, and myself third."

Trust is a gentle, fragile offshoot of faith. It begins when reason, or the intellect, folds its wings and allows the wings of faith to open up. For trust cannot exist without faith. If I have faith in a person, an institution, a family, I will trust. Wherever there is faith there is trust. It is very fragile and very beautiful.

The first person we need to trust is God, the Trinity. Do we question his ability to help us? We think that our everyday problems are our own problems, that we don't need faith or trust in God to solve them. We would prefer if at all possible to solve our own problems all the time. It gives us the sense of power, the sense of being our own master. We are willing to have God around and to trust him if and when it becomes quite evident that we cannot solve things by ourselves.

Trust demands the thrust of a lance into our hearts, leaving wide the wound of openness. (John 19:31–34) Since the Church came from the side of Christ, the bonds that unite us to Jesus Christ and his Mystical Body are always bonds of faith and trust.

Our contemporary generation may be smart and have vast experience but it has very little trust in the family, in marriage, in one another. We share the unimportant things but hide those that really matter.

To trust someone, and especially to trust the untrustworthy, doesn't seem at all sensible to us. Yet, this is exactly what Jesus Christ demands of us when he says: Pray for your enemies, love those who hate you. Give your life for your brothers, those who hate you and those who don't. (Luke 6:27–30) Very few of us have gone into the holocaust of his words, of trusting the untrustworthy.

With God, every moment is the moment of beginning again.

We are going to have to face despair in others. We will have to give them hope. How can we give hope if we don't pray? It is very draining to walk around the edge of despair. We Christians need to prepare ourselves for this. We exist to bring faith, hope, and love to the world.

Our preparation is to forget ourselves and be attentive and available to others.

    I live a life of constant unrelenting prayer, and also of fasting, that our selfishness and self-centeredness disappear before the luminous presence of God. My heart cries out to God unflaggingly, day and night, because a love blossoms forth from my heart, a love for everyone in the world. I am prostrated before God, asking him to have pity on us all, wherever we are.

    Hope makes us see that our worth is rooted in the incarnation, life, death, and resurrection of God. When we accept that, hope comes like an avalanche or like a fire, like a sauna of the Holy Spirit, and renews us. "Look," faith whispers, "it's not so tragic." With God every moment is the moment of beginning again.

    Let every day be the day of beginning again to love God back for all his love for us. Every day a little more. As my husband Eddie had inscribed on our wedding rings: "More than yesterday, less than tomorrow." Let every day be one of turning our face to God. For this, all we have to do is to look at the person next to us.

    God overcomes obstacles that no person could overcome. Out of weakness, defeat, and annihilation come forth rich fruits.

Chapter 19

Love

> You must love the Lord your God with all your heart, with all your soul, with all your mind and with all your strength... You must love your neighbour as yourself. There is no commandment greater than these.
>
> Mark 12:29-31

The mystery of iniquity and the mystery of love are confronting each other visibly, palpably, in the Church and in the world. Perhaps it is precisely because the fire of love is among us in so visible a manner that the anger of the Prince of Darkness is drawn forth.

In every city, every town, every village of the world, these two mysteries confront each other, simultaneously revealing the poverty and the wealth of Christians.

Is it any wonder, then, that those who do not believe in God obtain more reasons for their unbelief than ever before? For nothing repels people from religion more than the hypocrisy of those who give it only lip service.

But the problem is deeper than this visible appearance. Exactly why are there Christians who refuse others the justice and love which God demands of those who would enter his kingdom? Christian hearts which ought to be filled with love for everyone are often filled with hate. Christian hearts which are called to seek peace often talk and shout of war. Christian hearts which are commanded to worship but one God create for themselves a thousand other gods and live by values that do not even remotely resemble the gospel of Jesus Christ.

What are the reasons for this tragic state of affairs? Is it ignorance? How can that be? Our land is dotted with Catholic schools and universities. What is being taught there? Has Catholic education, Catholic training, Catholic formation been so negligent in teaching the essence of our faith, which is the commandment to love?

At a World Congress of the Laity held at the Vatican, the words of a woman from Cameroon etched themselves into my soul as if I had been branded with their fire. Simple, humble, yet positive and sure of what she had to say, she posed a question to the Christian Catholic West.

She said, "We the women of Cameroon, the mothers whom I represent, have a question. We bring our children up in the Catholic faith, teaching them to love and serve their neighbour and God. We are a poor nation, and you in your charity some years ago began to offer our children scholarships to your Catholic colleges. We were delighted to send our children to have their knowledge enlarged and to learn skills so they could help our country. Why is it, then, that most of them returned with hate in their hearts? Why have so many of them lost their faith?"

There was a moment of deep silence, since everyone knew that the roots of this "why" were in prejudice and in forgetting first things and prayer.

It is vital that we do not lose sight of the essence of our goal. Obstacles seem to nearly block out the fresh, invigorating wind that comes from the Holy Spirit.

We are reminded of the parable of Jesus concerning the exorcism of a certain person. A small group of evil spirits had been exorcised and the soul had been swept and made neat and tidy. But in some way the person did not keep up his vigilance. Before long his soul found itself again occupied, this time by an even greater hoard of evil spirits than before. (Luke 11:24–26)

Why is there so much rationalization, so much compromise? Perhaps one answer is that God permits it to happen so that we reexamine our consciences about his commandment of love, and begin to realize that there is a mystery of iniquity at work, a Prince of Darkness. Realizing this, we will begin anew to fight him by facing squarely the great reality of Christ, by taking up the weapons of prayer and fasting with which to exorcise Satan from our personal and national lives.

Remember that at times of confusion, bewilderment, pain, and fatigue, when our preconceived notions tumble down and when everything is bleak and dark, the Prince of Darkness will enter onto the scene. These are the colours of his domain. These are the times of his visitation. This is home to him. Do not fear his tactics. Make the sign of the cross, invoke the Mother of God, and use holy water. Simple, childlike remedies, but how potent. Above all, dwell in charity toward one another, for where love is, God is, and where God is, the Prince of Darkness vanishes.

Be alert and attentive to the voice of God.

God is present everywhere. But this is a time for realizing that Satan is on earth, too. Besides being prudent with the prudence of God, besides acknowledging and verbalizing one's human fears, besides praying for perseverance and courage, one has also to face Satan and face him fighting. He is fought with prayer, fasting, and mortification. He retreats speedily, as I said, before the sign of the cross, the invocation of the name of Jesus, and the calling upon Mary, the Mother of God.

We need to be alert and attentive to the voice of God. We Christians can become beacons of light, a hospice, an inn for pilgrims and seekers for God. The motley crowd that arrives at our doors is not simply motley but is composed of individuals in need of God. God has called us Christians to something very important, to be a place of refuge in the midst of a desert.

Forgiveness restores the bond of love.

Forgiveness is one of the urgent spiritual needs and actions of today. There is no use hiding behind rationalizations, no use sharpening our philosophical and theological arguments.

Now is the time to forgive. Begin with forgiving yourself. The Lord said, "Love your neighbour as yourself." (Matthew 22:39)

Which means we must love ourselves first. We need to begin with forgiving ourselves as our Father in heaven forgives us.

Simply, sincerely, and with grave humility we are to acknowledge our sins before ourselves. We go into the very depths of our souls and bring our faults out into the light. Then, after having begged forgiveness of them from God, we forgive ourselves.

We may have gone to confession, the sacrament of reconciliation, and been forgiven, but we remain uneasy, tragically still feeling guilty of those very sins we have just confessed to God and have been absolved from. We do not really trust either his love or his forgiveness.

Forgiveness is a very deep thing. To say, "I am sorry," is often said superficially. One needs to face the fact that one has wronged another person and go through a very great *kenosis* or emptying of self. To ask forgiveness is to make straight the path of the Lord, (John 1:23) and to face oneself with a heart that is pure. In this situation, a person has to humiliate himself. Then, pure of heart and open to being humiliated by himself, he can approach the humble Christ in his brother or sister with a real and deep sorrow, not a superficial thing, and really look at the ways he has hurt the other, meditate on them, and understand what he has done to the other.

Then, we go to the person, without any residual anger in some tiny corner of our heart, and really mean what we say when we apologize. But the Lord wants more. He wants you, while you are meditating on what you have done, to come to a great and beautiful love—not a "liking"—a love for the one you have offended, a love that will grow in your heart so that barriers will fall down.

Believe in his mercy and his erasure.

God does not want what has been forgiven to come back to haunt us or disturb us. One of the tragedies of this modern world is guilt. Our wrongdoings keep coming to mind. They accumulate like a hill, like a mountain sometimes, and crush us, even though we have asked forgiveness, even though we have gone to the great tribunal of mercy and forgiveness, the confessional. When God has erased, why do we remember? Christ is always reconciling us to himself. We need to believe in his mercy and in the fact of his erasure.

On the human level, it is the same. When you have hurt somebody, have approached that person, and have been forgiven, then it is erased. It is over with, done with. The bond of love has been restored, and there is no memory of the tragic moment of unloosing—which would stop you from loving further.

What a beautiful thing it is to be reconciled with a brother or sister. When we are truly reconciled with one another we can celebrate, with a celebration that is joyous and glad, full of laughter and song.

When someone on the wrong side of the ledger apologizes, there is also the fantastic joy of the one who forgives. It's a spontaneous gesture, a gesture of open arms. As the other person begins his apology, already he is embraced, already a new ring is placed on his finger and new clothes on his back, as it says in the gospel of the return of the prodigal son. (Luke 15:11–32) The father forgave, he ran forward, and so ought we. Whoever comes to us because they have done some hurt to us, if they apologize we are called to act as did the father of the prodigal son, but even more, as Christ constantly does to us. Then forgiveness becomes celebration.

Blessed are the merciful: they shall have mercy shown them.

We are called to love one another, and that means first forgiving ourselves and everybody else. In order to love, one needs to forgive. For one cannot love the object of hostility, anger, hatred, and unforgiveness. It may seem idiotic or irrelevant to speak about the command to love your neighbour as yourself (Matthew 22:39) by imploring everyone to begin with forgiving. Yet the world is in shambles. Greed is showing its face openly. Evil means are used to ensnare and subject one person to another. All dams seem to be breaking loose and the sticky, black waters of evil rising higher and higher across our cities and countries. In the face of all that, what is left but to talk about this command of the Lord? But that means forgiveness. That demands mercy and compassion. "Blessed are the merciful: they shall have mercy shown them." (Matthew 5:7)

Forgiveness can become an habitual state in which one forgives almost while one gets rejected, ignored, spat upon, or whatever. There is about this forgiveness business something divine, closely aligned to charity, to love, and to God. When we really love God, we need to activate that love by forgiving.

My forgiveness is given ahead of the deed, even as God grants it to all of us.

There is no need for forgiveness when one has forgiven well ahead of time, out of love. My forgiveness is given ahead of the deed, even as God grants it to all of us.

Mary, the Mother of God, shared her divine Son's passionate love for humanity, and she shared his pain. Our Lady's compassion bore the fruit of forgiveness. Her compassion and forgiveness bring healing to humanity. The incredible and incomprehensible love of God is filled with forgiveness. Because Mary accepted to share Christ's love, pain, and forgiveness, she became the Mother of us all, and people understand that they cannot walk through life without her, in a manner of speaking.

It is true that forgiveness, mercy, and compassion may and probably will lead to that other truth uttered by Christ, "No one can have greater love than to lay down his life for his friends." (John 15:13) But wouldn't it be wonderful to die trying to forgive and love, rather than to die with hatred in one's heart?

Let us ask Mary, the Mother of God and of all humanity, who loved and forgave those who killed her Son, to teach us how to pray, how to love, how to forgive.

About the Author

Catherine Kolyschkine was born into an aristocratic family in Russia in 1896, and baptized in the Russian Orthodox Church. Because of her father's work, she grew up in Ukraine, Egypt, and Paris. Many different strands of Christianity were woven into the spiritual fabric of her family background, but it was from the liturgy of the Russian Orthodox Church, the living faith of her father and mother, and the earthy piety of the Russian people themselves that Catherine received the powerful spiritual traditions and symbols of the Christian East.

At fifteen Catherine was married to Boris de Hueck. Soon they were swept into World War I, where she served as a nurse at the front. After the Revolution of 1917 they endured with all the peoples of the Russian Empire the agonies of starvation and civil war. Eventually Catherine and Boris escaped to England. At the beginning of her new life in the West, Catherine embraced the teachings of the Roman Catholic Church, without rejecting the spiritual wealth of her Orthodox heritage.

In 1921 the couple sailed to Canada where, shortly after their arrival in Toronto, Catherine gave birth to their son George. As refugees, they experienced dire poverty for a few years—but soon Catherine's intelligence, energy, and gift for public speaking brought her to the attention of a large lecture bureau. Her talks were popular all across Canada and the United States. Within a few years, she became an executive with another, international lecture service. She became a North American success story.

In the 1930's, after several years of anguish, Catherine and Boris separated permanently; later the Church annulled their marriage. As devastated as Catherine was, she knew that God wanted something new from her now, but she did not know what it was. The words of Christ haunted her: "Sell all you possess, and give it to the poor, and come, follow Me." She consulted the archbishop of Toronto about her new vocation, and he eventually blessed it.

Catherine took a room in a slum section of Toronto and began to quietly love and serve her neighbours, becoming their friend, and praying, hidden in their midst. Her example of radical Gospel living became a magnet for men and women in search of a way to live their faith. Catherine had not envisaged a community, but when the Archbishop told her that, yes, Christ was calling her to this, she accepted, and soon Friendship House was born.

The works of Friendship House were modest—a shelter for the homeless, meals for the hungry, recreation and books for the young, a newspaper to make known the social teachings of the Church. In 1938 Catherine initiated an interracial apostolate in Harlem, New York, living with and serving the African-Americans. This work expanded to other cities: Chicago, Washington, D.C., and Portland, Oregon. Friendship House became well known in the American Church.

Catherine shared with her friend, Dorothy Day of the Catholic Worker, the intense struggle to move the Gospel out of books and into believers' lives. Even if a few friends, such as the young Thomas Merton, recognized in her the power of the Holy Spirit and an unwavering fidelity to Christ's Church, many others were frightened by her Russian bluntness. Others simply could not grasp the largeness of her vision, especially because her experience of the ways of God were so foreign to them. Finally after a painful difference of opinion over the nature of the Friendship House apostolate, Catherine found herself pushed again into the chartless waters of the Lord.

This time Catherine did not have to start alone. In 1943 she had married Eddie Doherty, a celebrated American newspaperman of Irish descent, after he convinced her and her bishop that he wanted to share and support her vocation. In 1947, then, Catherine and Eddie came to Combermere, a small village northeast of Toronto, where the Bishop of Pembroke had agreed she could work among the rural families.

What seemed like the end of the road turned out to be the most fruitful period of Catherine's life. The community of Madonna House was born, and grew into an open family of lay men, lay women, and priests, living in love and breathing from the "two lungs," East and West, of the Catholic Church. As Catherine's inner life deepened and the community matured, she shared the fullness of the inner vocation Christ had formed in her. Over the years Catherine authored dozens of books; her award-winning book, *Poustinia: Encountering God in Silence, Solitude and Prayer*, was hailed as "a modern spiritual classic" and translated into many languages.

Today, the Madonna House Apostolate continues to grow. It currently has more than 200 members, including more than twenty priests, and has foundations in Europe, Russia, Africa, South America and West Indies, in addition to the many in Canada and the United States. The training center in Combermere, Ontario offers an experience of Gospel life to guests who come to participate fully in the community life. In the Madonna House way of life are the seeds of a new Christian civilization.

Catherine Doherty died on December 14, 1985—a woman who had become a spiritual giant by responding to grace. The cause for her canonization has been officially opened in the Catholic Church.

More information about Catherine's life, works, and the progress of her cause can be found on the Internet at: www.catherinedoherty.org

Catherine Doherty's world-renowned spiritual classic

Poustinia, a Russian word, means "desert," a place to meet Christ in silence, solitude and prayer. In this important book, Catherine Doherty combines her insights into the great spiritual traditions of the Russian Church with her very personal experience of life with Christ.

Catherine emphasizes "poustinia of the heart," an interiorized poustinia, a silent chamber carried always and everywhere within which to contemplate God. One's desert can be in the marketplace, in the midst of countless conferences, traffic jams, bus trips—or a hospital ward.

A timeless best-seller, published in 16 foreign editions, *Poustinia* won the prestigious French Academy Award. The experience of poustinia has become a worldwide phenomenon following its publicity through this popular book.

"Classics are rarer than precious gems, so it is a delight to discover a new one... One finds a refreshing and startling Christian authenticity in Doherty's writing..."
— *Christian Century*

"This is a rare and beautiful book. It reveals a way of entering into deeper knowledge of the indwelling Presence of God, by someone who has been there."
— *The Franciscan*

Paperback edition:
$13.95 U.S. • $17.50 Canadian
210 pgs. • 5½ x 8¼ trade pbk.
ISBN 0-921440-54-5

AudioBook edition:
$24.95 U.S. • $34.95 Canadian
5½ hours • 4 cassettes
ISBN 0-921440-53-7

***Poustinia* is also available on cassette in AudioBook format**

Read by Father Émile Brière—a pioneer priest of the Madonna House Apostolate, a poustinik himself, and a close friend of the author.

ORDER TOLL FREE: 1-888-703-7110

A REFRESHING DAILY SPIRITUAL DEVOTIONAL

Meditations that will inspire you every day of the year

This seasonal devotional features meditations drawn from the down-to-earth and eminently practical writings of Catherine Doherty.

Providing daily spiritual guidance, there are deep insights on prayer and spiritual growth as well as homespun words of advice on everyday work and family life. Nostalgic entries even recall Christmas and Easter customs from Catherine's childhood in the old Russia of the czars.

"A sampling of daily topics evokes their richness and variety:

- A Remedy for Pain: Forgiveness
- What Christ Asks of Us
- What Happens When You Take The Risk
- Superficial Communications and Loneliness
- The Gospel is Risky Business
- A Meditation on Yelling

Because *Grace in Every Season* lives up to its title, it also makes a wonderful spiritual gift for any occasion: Christmas, birthday, graduation, wedding, or anniversary."

— Larry Holley, *The Pecos Benedictine*

$14.95 U.S. • $18.75 Canadian • 320 pages
5½ x 8¼ trade pbk. • ISBN 0-921440-31-6

"I recommend this book to anyone who wishes to follow the Lord Jesus more closely. The writings of Catherine Doherty help us all to live the gospel 'without compromise.' Mary Bazzett has done a great service in arranging Catherine's writings for daily prayer and reflection.'"

— James Cardinal Hickey

"The writings of Catherine Doherty belong in the realm of contemporary classics. With this book of seasonal selections, we have ready-at-hand some of her most memorable reflections on the mysteries of our faith as well as personal accounts of her profound prayer experiences. I heartily recommend it for all Christians."

— Susan Muto, author *Pathways to Living*

ORDER TOLL FREE: 1-888-703-7110

Madonna House Publications
Combermere • Ontario • Canada

"Lord, give bread to the hungry, and hunger for you to those who have bread," was a favourite prayer of our foundress, Catherine Doherty. At Madonna House Publications, we strive to satisfy the spiritual hunger for God in our modern world with the timeless words of the Gospel message.

Faithful to the teachings of the Catholic Church and its magisterium, Madonna House Publications is a non-profit apostolate dedicated to publishing high quality and easily accessible books, audiobooks, videos and music. We pray our publications will awaken and deepen in our readers an experience of Jesus' love in the most simple and ordinary facets of everyday life.

Your generosity can help Madonna House Publications provide the poor around the world with editions of important spiritual works containing the enduring wisdom of the Gospel message. If you would like to help, please send your contribution to the address below. We also welcome your questions and comments. May God bless you for your participation in this apostolate.

Madonna House Publications
2888 Dafoe Rd
Combermere ON   K0J 1L0
Canada

Internet: www.madonnahouse.org/publications
E-mail: publications@madonnahouse.org
Telephone: (613) 756-3728